Signature Tastes
of
VANCOUVER

SMOKE ALARM
MEDIA

To the incomparable Jennifer Colvin-Slinger. By a wide margin, you are the most intelligent woman I have ever had the distinct pleasure to know. And it's not even your strongest point.

To Michaela and Danica. Continue in the example that your mother has set, and you will continue to become the great women you were meant to be.

And to Karla...Thank you for taking Jen fishing, even if for a few days.

To this beautiful city to our north, that represents the right way in so many ways...Perhaps you might let me stay permanently.

Welcome to Vancouver: City of Glass photography from the Canadian Archives

To others unnamed, because my memory is as short as my hair.

You can find us at www.signaturetastes.com and on Facebook: Smoke Alarm Media

Layout by Steven W. Siler

Photography by Rosalie Anne Fradella and team, except where noted

Library of Congress Control Number: 2010914234

Siler, Steven W.

Signature Tastes of Vancouver: Favorite Recipes from our Local Restaurants

ISBN 978-1-927458-02-0

1. Restaurants-Canada-Vancouver-Guidebooks. 2. Cookery-Canada-Vancouver

Printed in the United States of America and Canada

This book is dedicated to the emergency responders...

From the first frantic call to 9-1-1
To the comforting hands at Harborside
You give your time...

away from spouses,
away from friends,
away from children,
and yes, even from meals...

To assure all of us:

"Tonight, I will make it better for you
no matter what,
I will watch over you..."

I have always wondered if anyone really reads the Table of Contents. Now since this is a cookbook, I should have organized everything under its proper heading, like soups, pasta, desserts and the like. This is not just a cookbook as much as a Culinary Postcard; a celebration of the city itself...about the eateries, fine dining, casual dining, bars, drive -ins, and of course, the people.

Welcome to Vancouver: City of Glass..7

The Eateries...

CITY OF GLASS

Signature Tastes of VANCOUVER

"To describe the beauties of this region, will, on some future occasion, be a very grateful task to the pen of a skilled panegyrist..."

George Vancouver to the Admirality, 1792

Welcome to Vancouver! This coastal city on the mainland of British Columbia – or BC – in Canada is home to over 603,000 people, which, though that might not sound like a huge number, ranks it as the eighth-largest Canadian city, and one of the most densely populated Canadian municipalities. It is also one of the most ethnically and linguistically diverse cities in Canada; of its residents, over 50% speak English as their second -- or third or fourth or… -- language, and 35% of its population is not

Canadian-born. Vancouver also has the highest percentage of Asian residents in any North American city – it's sometimes referred to as HongCouver -- a fact that definitely calls for a stop in their version of Chinatown, one of the oldest and largest in

WELCOME TO VANCOUVER
STACEY BREITBERG, EDITOR-AT-LARGE

North America.

According to archaeological findings, the current Vancouver area was settled by the Coast Salish people as early as BC 500, long before the first permanent non-native settlement – called Gastown – which sprang up around the Hastings Mill logging sawmill and a neighboring tavern that were both established in 1867. This settlement grew to become a small town called Granville, until 1886, when the city was incorporated and renamed Vancouver, after the British naval captain George Vancouver who had explored the area in the late 18th century. Three months later – on June 16th, 1886 – a serious fire destroyed much of the city, but it was quickly rebuilt. By 1887, the transcontinental railway was extended to reach the city and its large, advantageous natural seaport, and soon Vancouver was prospering as a vital

part of the trade route between the Orient, London, and Eastern Canada. Today, Port Metro Vancouver is still the largest and busiest port in all of Canada, and one of the most diverse in North America. National Geographic claims that the term "skid row" might have originated here in the 1800s, when areas currently oc-

Some of the old growth trees
harvested from the area.

cupied by the city of Vancouver were mostly un-populated forests. Wooden skids were built – in the area that is now East Hastings – to move logs being dumped in the Burrard Inlet so they could be floated to the Hastings sawmill. When those areas eventually became the "seedier" parts of the city, skid row was – possibly – born. Today, how-ever, Vancouver consistently ranks as one of the top ten most liveable cities in the entire world. It is one of the only North American cities with no downtown freeways – though it has many large walking promenades along its waterfront. It is also full of well-maintained public parks, including Stanley Park, which borders the city and is 10% bigger than New York City's Central Park.

Vancouver is sometimes referred to as "Hollywood North", placing third – behind only Los Angeles and New York City – in North American feature film production, due to a combination of its consistently mild climate, the diversity of its neighbor-hoods and landscapes, and its favorable film industry tax concessions. Three major film companies -- Lions Gate, Bridge and Paramount – have studios here, and each year brings the production of new films, such as Twilight: New Moon, Legends of

the Fall, X2, Fantastic Four, Fear, Alive, and The Accused, as well as the television show Supernatural.

Vancouver is home to a wide array of fantastic restaurants, with more new options per capita opening their doors each year than most other large cities on the conti-

nent, and its residents are well aware of this; Vancou-verites dine out more than the residents of any other North American city. Also, proving the "nice Canadian" stereo-type that everyone in the US seems to have, Vancouverites are notoriously good tippers – to everyone from baristas, bartenders, restaurant servers, and taxi drivers.

Whether you're looking for fresh-from-the-ocean seafood, some authentic Chinese cuisine, late-night pizza, a multi-course dinner, or an afternoon snack, you'll find

more options than you'll have room for, even if you've spent the day working up an ap-petite. Luckily, there are sev-eral well-used ski hills within an easy drive of the city, occa-sional dolphin and whale sightings in the nearby wa-ters – last year, for example, there were two whale sightings in False Creek and quite a few dolphin pods sighted in Howe Sound – and nearby mountain hiking trails, making it easy to combine outdoor adventures with your culinary explorations: have breakfast before heading up for a morning ski run in Whistler, a seafood lunch

at Granville Island after a whale watching trip, or a restorative dinner at a mountaintop restaurant after a hike. And if you're looking for something to toast with after a long day spent soaking up the sights, you're in luck – there are all kinds of local breweries, wineries, and distilleries in the area, so you will be sure to find the

perfect microbrew, glass of wine, or single-malt whisky to sip.

Vancouver also boasts a variety of farmers markets – most of which operate from late-spring through late-fall, plus one winter market that runs from the fall through the early spring – and the mild climate ensures there will always be something delicious and locally-grown on offer. Its various markets also host many different annual festivals throughout the year – the Garden Festival in May, the Bike Festival in June, the Berry Festival in July, a grand Picnic In The Park in early August, the Corn Festival in late August, the Tomato Festival in September, and the Harvest Festival in October.

Vancouver has one of the largest gay communities in the West, so don't forget to check out the summertime gay pride parade and all of its festivities.

Finally, once your trip has drawn to a close, you'll find a convenient gas station

practically next door to the Vancouver airport, ideal for refilling the tank of your rental car before you drop it off – and its gas prices are competitive, not a price-of-convenience rip-off. It's that kind of trademark Canadian niceness that will surely have you coming back for another visit soon.

Signature Tastes of VANCOUVER

WELCOME TO VANCOUVER

STACEY BREITBERG, EDITOR-AT-LARGE

GOCANU

Malhotra's Stanley Cup dream in jeopardy. » F1

Five wa to fix Canu » F2

THE VA

BREAKING NEWS | VANCOUVERSUN.COM

Libs, NDP ha

Hundreds of Surrey residents

organizers for candidates
both parties were aggressively
up South Asians in
leadership

RECIPES
&
RESTAURANTS

BC Spot Prawn Risotto with Garden Fresh Peas, Sautéed Pea Tendrils and Olive Oil

100 Nights, if you haven't been keeping track, is the follow-up to 100 Days, a pop-up restaurant opened in the Opus Hotel last year – for a mere 100 days – while plans were developed for a permanent venue. Well, 100 Days was such a hit that management decided to keep things going and morph it into 100 Nights. The concept has stayed pretty much the same. The restaurant is a unique combination of upscale and unfinished – classy and gritty all at once.

Ingredients:
1 lemon
4 C. (1 L) water
2 lbs. (1 kg) fresh B.C. spot prawns
4 C. (1 L) cooked risotto rice, as per package instructions
1 C. (250 mL) fish stock
1 C. (250 mL) parmesan cheese
salt and pepper to taste
1 lb. (450g) pea tendrils
1 tbsp. (15 mL) garlic
2 tbsp. (30 mL) salted butter
2 C. (500 mL) fresh green peas
2 tbsp. (30 mL) olive oil

Instructions:
1. Boil water with lemon that has been juiced and cut in half. Tear the heads off the spot prawns, place in a large bowl and pour boiling water over top of tails to cover. Leave the prawns in water for 45 seconds to cook. Remove from water and let stand on counter to cool a bit, then peel.

2. Pre-cook the risotto to package specifications, as each type of arborio rice cooking methods vary from brand to brand. Mix the risotto with half the fish stock adding more and more stock until you have the right consistency, add the cheese and season with salt and pepper. Sauté the pea tendrils with the garlic and butter then add to the risotto. Add the peas. Heat and serve.

3. For each serving, place ¼ of the finished risotto into a dinner bowl and ¼ of the peeled prawns on top of the risotto, drizzle with olive oil.

100 NIGHTS AT OPUS HOTEL
322 DAVIE STREET, VANCOUVER, BC

"Part of the secret of success in life is to eat what you like and let the food fight it out inside."
Mark Twain

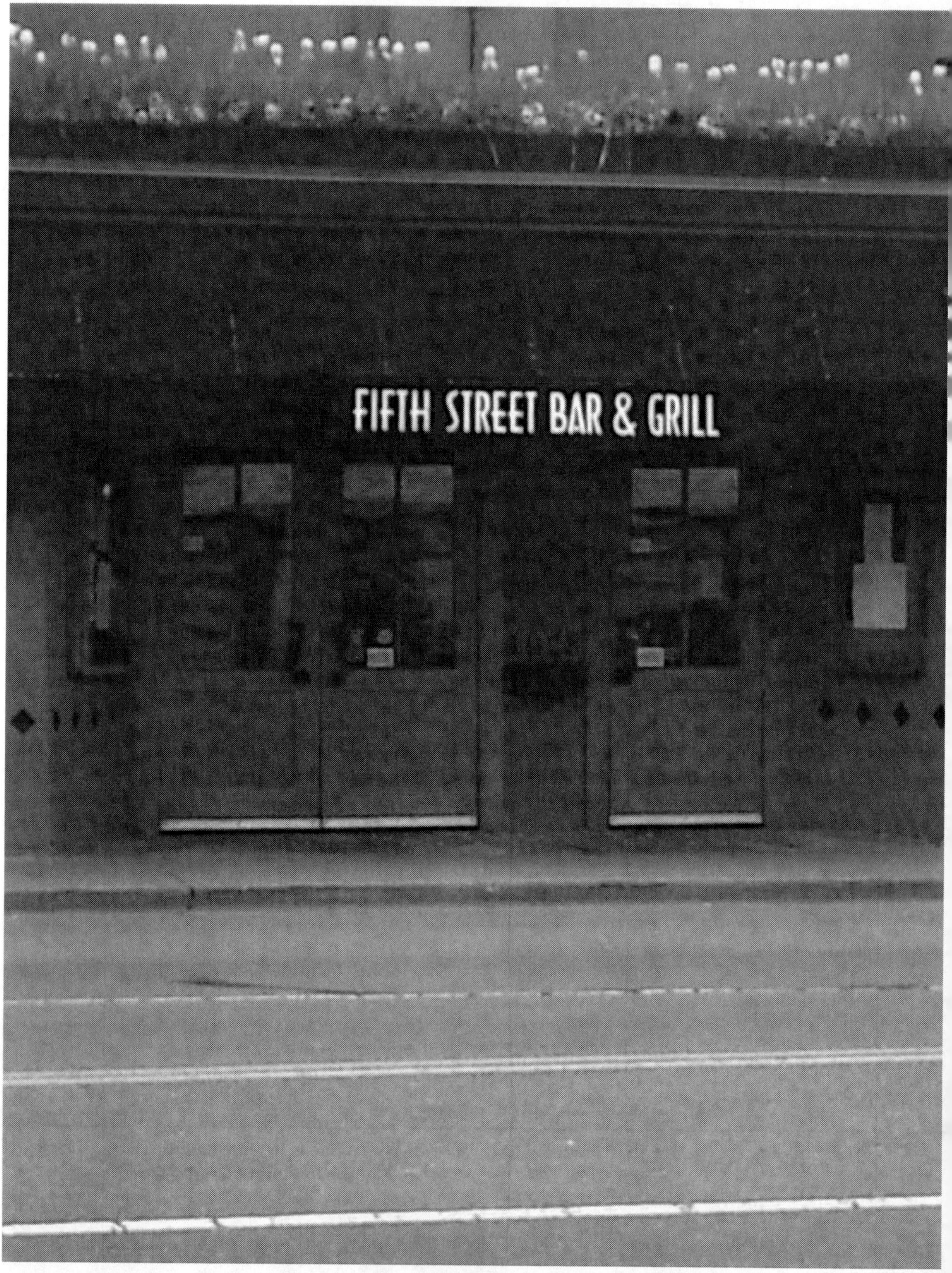
FIFTH STREET BAR & GRILL

Signature Tastes of VANCOUVER

Featuring beautifully crafted woodwork, original artwork, and the textured charm of tile and brick, 5th Street Bar & Wood Fired Grill boasts one of Vancouver Island's few wood-fired rotisseries. Gas fireplaces on our two patios create a cozy European ambiance for savouring luscious pastas and gourmet pizzas. Signature dishes include spit-roasted chicken, rotisserie smoked meats, juicy steaks, grilled ribs, as well as daily features that include fresh seafood.

Ingredients:
little Qualicum Brie cheese wheel
cornmeal
roast garlic confit (pureed garlic and vegetable oil)
mixed greens
artichokes
sundried tomatoes
fresh chopped basil
toasted pine nuts or sliced almonds
warmed balsamic vinaigrette

Instructions:
1. Slice sundried tomatoes and artichoke hearts and lightly tossing them with mixed greens and freshly chopped basil.
2. Garnish the salad with toasted almonds or pine nuts, placing it in a bowl or plate and including the warmed balsamic vinaigrette on the side.

To Prepare the Cheese:
1. Cut the Brie wheel horizontally into 1-inch slices. Then cover one side of the slice with the roasted garlic confit and then press cornmeal on top of it.
2. Place the Brie, cornmeal side down, on a hot pan with a small amount of vegetable oil. Sear the cheese for 1-2 minutes until it's lightly browned, and then place it on top of the mixed green salad.

5TH STREET BAR AND GRILL
1028 HILLSIDE AVE, VICTORIA, BC

"A good meal makes a man feel more charitable toward the whole world than any sermon."
Arthur Pendenys

LEMON HOLLANDAISE

Signature Tastes of VANCOUVER

Located just up Yew Street from Kits Beach, Abigail's Party is a popular, fun, and stylish spot boasting a brunch card with top-drawer huevos rancheros. Today, Jesse Grasso, Chef de Cuisine is here to dish up some favourites!

Ingredients:
4 free range egg yolks
8 oz. clarified butter
juice of 1 lemon
salt and pepper to taste
dash of tabasco

Instructions:
1. Bring a small pot of water to a boil - use a pot that your mixing bowl will fit over.
2. Place egg yolks in mixing bowl and whisk lightly.
3. Place bowl over simmering water and whisk vigorously until semi stiff ribbons start to form – this should take approximately 3 minutes (be very careful not to scramble your eggs - if it looks like the eggs are getting too hot, remove the bowl from the pot and whisk off the heat for a few seconds.
4. Once you get to the ribbon stage, remove the bowl from heat and slowly add your butter while continuing to whisk until the desired consistency is achieved (add less butter for a thinner hollandaise, or the full amount for a more rich/thick hollandaise).
5. Add lemon juice, salt & pepper and Tabasco to taste.
6. Hold the sauce in a warm area and use within one hour.

1651-1699 YEW STREET, VANCOUVER, BC

ABIGAIL'S

"If life throws you a lemon - make lemonade."
Joan Collins

SHRIMP MELT

Acme Cafe, which opened at 51 West Hastings, is one of the first of this newest new wave. That it experienced line-ups in its first few days is a pretty good indication that there's a market for more in these parts. That it happens to be good only raises the bar for whomever and whatever comes next.

Ingredients:
¼ C. butter
1 tbsp. chopped green onion
1 lb. fresh shrimp, peeled and deveined
2 tbsps. all-purpose flour
2 tbsps. Old Bay Seasoning TM
2 C. milk
1 tbsp. celery, chopped
1 large tomato, sliced
8 slices provolone cheese
4 English muffins, split and toasted

Instructions:

1. In a medium saucepan, melt butter and saute onions and shrimp over medium heat until shrimp are pink.

2. Stir in flour and Old Bay seasoning to make a roux. Slowly pour in milk, stirring constantly. Allow to thicken. Stir in celery and cook until celery is soft.

3. Preheat oven on broiler setting.

4. Spoon mixture over toasted English muffins, top each with a slice of tomato and provolone cheese. Place under a preheated broiler for 30 seconds to 1 minute or until cheese is melted.

51 WEST HASTINGS STREET, VANCOUVER, BC

ACME CAFE

"A good cook is like a sorceress who dispenses happiness."
Elsa Schiapirelli

ROASTED ASPARAGUS SALAD

Adesso, in Italian means now, now as in modern, now as in today, now as in current. Our menu and our daily specials reflect today's trend towards healthy, local and seasonal organic foods. At Adesso Bistro we take a modern approach to the traditional cuisine of Italy's Ligurian region, a... refreshing return to food made with love, tradition and soul. Our goal is to create an experience for our guests that will capture the essence of Adesso's unique regional cuisine.

Ingredients:
1½ lbs. fresh asparagus
½ C. olive oil, divided
1½ tbsp. chopped fresh basil, divided
½ tsp. lemon pepper
½ tsp. salt, divided
¼ C. balsamic vinegar
1 garlic clove, minced
1 C. halved cherry tomatoes (about ½ pt.)
½ C. chopped red bell pepper
¼ C. finely chopped red onion
1 head bibb lettuce, torn into bite-size pieces
1 avocado, sliced

Instructions:
1. Preheat oven to 425°. Snap off and discard tough ends of asparagus; remove scales with a vegetable peeler, if desired.
2. Stir together 1 tablespoon olive oil, 1½ teaspoon chopped basil, ½ teaspoon lemon pepper, and ¼ teaspoon salt in a large bowl.
3. Add asparagus to olive oil mixture, and toss gently to coat. Place asparagus on a lightly greased baking sheet.
4. Bake asparagus at 425° for 13 to 15 minutes or to desired degree of tenderness. Cool 10 minutes.
5. Whisk together balsamic vinegar, garlic, and remaining 7 tablespoons olive oil, 1 tablespoon basil, and ¼ teaspoon salt.
6. Toss together tomatoes, bell pepper, onion, and 1 tablespoon balsamic vinegar mixture.
7. Arrange lettuce on individual serving plates. Top with tomato mixture and asparagus. Add avocado just before serving. Drizzle with remaining balsamic vinegar mixture.

Note: To make ahead, toss together tomatoes, bell pepper, and onion without dressing. Store these ready-to-use ingredients in an airtight container in the refrigerator up to five hours. The dressing and asparagus can also be made up to eight hours before serving.

1906 HARO STREET, VANCOUVER, BC

ADESSO BISTRO

"Let food be thy medicine and medicine be thy food"
Hippocrates

EDAMAME

Since summer 2006, new owners Raya Audet & Nigel Springthorpe have been quietly turning the Alibi Room into the place for local craft beer on tap. We have become a true Free House, pouring guest beers from all over the province and beyond. Head chef Greg Armstrong has added an understated sophistication to our very accessible menu. The menu reflects a strong desire to provide familar, comforting dishes with an emphasis on quality ingredients.

Ingredients:
2 tbsp. toasted sesame seeds
½ tsp. coarse salt
1 lb. frozen edamame, in pods

Instructions:
1. Coarsely grind sesame seeds and salt in a spice grinder, then place in a small bowl. (Alternatively, chop sesame seeds and salt together finely.)

2. Fill a large pot fitted with a steamer insert or basket with 2 to 3 inches water. Bring water to a simmer over medium-high heat. Steam edamame, covered, until hot, 3 to 4 minutes. Transfer to a bowl, and sprinkle with sesame-salt mixture. Serve immediately.

Signature Tastes of VANCOUVER

157 ALEXANDER STREET, VANCOUVER, BC

ALIBI ROOM

"A good meal ought to begin with hunger."
French proverb

Linguine alla Carbonara

With only three sauces and a four burner electric stove, Tony started small. The "old" Anton's Pasta, established in 1983, consisted of nine tables and one very dedicated man. When Tony opened Vancouver's original pasta bar his vision was simple: good food at an affordable price and lots of it! The word was out. It was hard, even for the hungriest of people, to finish the huge portions served up at Anton's Pasta. If you did finish your plate, Tony went out of his way to ensure you left feeling full and satisfied.

Ingredients:
¼ C. extra-virgin olive oil
1 tbsp. unsalted butter
1 yellow onion, minced
4 oz. pancetta or prosciutto, diced
1 lb. fresh linguine
3 large egg yolks, at room temperature
½ C. heavy cream, at room temperature
¾ C. finely grated Parmigiano-Reggiano, at room temperature
freshly ground black pepper

Instructions:
1. Heat oil and butter in a large saute pan over medium heat. Add the onion and pancetta and cook until the onions are translucent and the pancetta is beginning to crisp. Remove from the heat and set aside.

2. Bring a large pot of salted water to a boil and cook the linguine according to package directions until al dente, about 2 to 3 minutes. Drain pasta in a colander (reserve a small amount of the cooking liquid in a small bowl) and return pasta to the pot. Return the pot to the heat and add the reserved pancetta and onion mixture. Stir over high heat until pasta is coated with the pancetta mixture.

3. In a bowl, whisk together the egg yolks and heavy cream and add to the pasta, along with the Parmesan. Remove the pot from the heat and toss the pasta until it is well-coated. Season with salt and freshly ground black pepper, to taste. If needed, add a bit of the reserved pasta cooking liquid to help toss the pasta if it is dry. Serve immediately.

Anton's Pasta Bar
4260 East Hastings Street, Burnaby, BC

"Food, like a loving touch or a glimpse of divine power, has that ability to comfort."
Norman Kolpas

Spot Prawn Tortelloni with English Peas and Lemon Thyme

The culinary cornerstone in the heart of Whistler Village, Araxi enjoys a long-held international reputation for excellence in food, wine and hospitality. The dining room resonates with lively ambiance enhanced with fresh flowers and original works of art. The adjoining Bar is the mountain's popular gathering place for locals and visitors, and in the summer season the patio is the nexus of Whistler's village life, wrapped by stunning mountain vistas.

Ingredients:

Spot Prawn Tortelloni:
1 lb. spot prawns, peeled and shells reserved for sauce, well chilled
4 oz. wild salmon, skin and bones removed, well chilled
1½ tsp. kosher salt
¼ tsp. freshly grated nutmeg
juice and zest of 1 lemon
1 egg
1 tbsp. brandy
3 tbsp. whipping cream
1 tsp. chopped fresh dill
1 recipe fresh pasta dough
1 tbsp. olive oil

Lemon Thyme Sauce and Peas:
2 shallots, minced
1 tbsp. unsalted butter
6 tbsp. vermouth
reserved prawn shells
1 C. fish stock
3 springs thyme
⅓ C. whipping cream
¾ cup shucked fresh peas, 4 whole pods reserved
¼ grated pecorino Romano cheese

Instructions:

Prawn Tortelloni:

1. Chill the bowl of a food processor and a stainless steel bowl in the refrigerator for 30 minutes. Place the spot prawns and salmon in the food processor bowl and pulse until the seafood is chopped and well combined. Add the salt, nutmeg, lemon juice and lemon zest and pulse again to combine. Add the egg and process at high speed until well mixed, about 2 minutes. Transfer the mixture to the chilled stainless steel bowl and fold in the brandy, followed by the cream and the dill. Refrigerate the prawn filling while you roll out the pasta.

2. Lightly moisten a tea towel with cold water. Following the instructions on your pasta machine, roll the dough into a sheet the thickness of a dime. Using a round cutter or a glass, cut the dough into twenty-four 3½- to 4-inch/9- to 10-cm rounds. Assemble the rounds in a stack and cover them with the damp cloth.

3. Lightly dust a baking sheet with flour and fill a small bowl with water. Fill a large roasting pan with ice. Place the bowl of prawn filling on the ice while you work with the dough.

4. Place one pasta round on a clean work surface. Spoon 2 tsp/10 mL of the filling onto the centre of the pasta, then, using a pastry brush, lightly brush the edges of the round with water. Fold the top half of the pasta round over the bottom half to form a semi-circle, being careful to completely enclose the filling.

5. To shape the tortelloni, lay a pasta semi-circle—flat edge toward you—across the middle of your index finger. There should be an even amount of pasta on both sides of your finger. Dab a small amount of water on one corner of the semi-circle, then fold the pasta around your finger, bringing the two tips together. With the thumb and fore- finger of your other hand, press the tips together tightly to seal the tortelloni, then carefully slide it off your finger. Place this tortelloni on the baking sheet, and continue filling and shaping the remaining tortelloni until you have used up all the pasta and the filling. Reserve the pasta while you prepare the sauce. Will keep refrigerated, covered with plastic wrap, for 1 day.

Lemon Thyme Sauce and Peas Sauce:

1. Place the shallots and butter in a small saucepan on low heat and sauté until softened but not coloured, about 5 minutes. Increase the heat to medium, add the vermouth and reduce until almost all the liquid has evaporated, about 8 minutes. Add the prawn shells and cook for 5 minutes, or until the shells redden from the heat. Reduce the heat to medium-low, stir in the fish stock and 1 sprig of lemon thyme and simmer until the liquid is reduced by half, about 10 minutes. Pour in the cream, remove from the heat and cover the pot with a lid or plastic wrap. Allow the sauce to infuse for 30 minutes.

2. Strain the sauce through a fine-mesh sieve into a clean saucepan and discard the solids. Bring the sauce to a simmer on medium heat and add the shucked peas. Cook for 3 minutes, then remove from the heat.

Finish Prawn Tortelloni:

1. Bring a large pot of water to a boil on high heat. Add about 1 tsp/5 mL of salt per 4 cups/1 L of water. Add the tortelloni and cook for 3 to 4 minutes. To check for doneness, cut a tortelloni in half and look to see if the edges of the dough are cooked. Using a slotted spoon, transfer the tortelloni to a bowl and drizzle with the olive oil.

TO SERVE:

1. Place 5 or 6 tortelloni in each bowl and cover with sauce. Split open the whole peapods to expose the peas and arrange a pod on each serving. Sprinkle each serving with pecorino Romano cheese and lemon thyme leaves. Serve immediately. Serves 4.

Araxi Restaurant + Bar
4222 Village Square, Whistler, BC

Caprese Salad

"Deep Cove is a crowd of discerning, food loving folks in flip flops" The Georgia Strait "This Bistro is one of those local gems that foodies like me dream of discovering but dread revealing for fear of exposing its virtuous flavours" Cathy Bullen "Simply Devine" The North Shore News.

Ingredients:
*2 large ball of fresh mozzarella (also known as mozzarella fior di latte), sliced ¼ in. thick
4 ripe roma tomatoes, sliced ¼ in. thick
10-12 sweet basil leaves, washed and patted dry
good quality extra virgin olive oil for drizzling
sea salt and freshly ground black pepper to taste*

Instructions:
1. On a large platter arrange tomato and mozzarella slices and basil leaves, alternating and overlapping them.

2. Sprinkle salad with a little salt and pepper.

3. Drizzle with a little olive oil and serve.

Arms Reach Bistro
4390 Gallant Avenue #107C, North Vancouver, BC

"Vulgarity is the garlic in the salad of life."
Cyril Connolly

"Moules aux Pernod" (Mussels in Pernod)

Overlooking the 55 acres vineyard of Domaine de Chaberton Estate Winery, the Zagat rated 'Excellent' Bacchus Bistro serves authentic French Bistro cuisines prepared with local ingredients and a West Coast flair. Rated by the Vancouver Sun newspaper as one of the top 3 'al Fresco' dining restaurants in Vancouver, the seasonal patio is truly the place to enjoy fine dining, 100% BC wines and seasonal cuisine. The "à la carte" menu is joined by a daily table d'hôte menu where Executive Chef Ashley's culinary prowess showcases what the local seasonal market places have to offer. As an added bonus, the table d'hôte menu offers a suggested wine pairing from the complete selection of Chaberton and Canoe Cove wines.

Ingredients:
1lb. fresh Mussels (we use salt spring island mussel when available)
5 cloves garlic, crushed
1 medium onion, sliced
1 bulb fennel, whites sliced, green fronds reserved
1 oz. pernod
1 C. heavy cream
¼ C. (approx.) of dry white wine
1 tbsp. butter
1 lemon
1 bunch parsley, chopped

Instructions:
1. Heat enough butter to generously cover the bottom of a large heavy pot. Add the garlic, onion, shallot and sliced fennel.
2. Gently cook, without colouring the onions, until slightly transluscent. Add the Pernod, (off the heat, safety first!) and 'flame' off the alcohol.
3. Now add the mussels, white wine, and cream.
4. Season with salt and pepper to taste. Stir well, cover with lid. Cook on medium heat until the mussels open, stiring frequently.
5. Finish the sauce with a knob of butter, a squeeze of fresh lemon, the chopped parsley and fennel fronds.
6. Stir to incorporate. Adjust seasoning, if necessary, and serve immediately with a side of crusty bread.
7. Pairs well with Domaine de Chaberton Unoaked Chardonnay or Bacchus.

Signature Tastes of VANCOUVER

1064 216 St Domaine de Chaberton, Langley, BC

Bacchus Bistro

"Nearly everyone wants as least one outstanding meal a day."
Duncan Hines

PISANG GORENG

Prepare to step out of Vancouver and into the warm heart of Malaysia at the award-winning Banana Leaf Malaysian Cuisine. Our cheerful atmosphere, friendly service, colourful traditional decor, and excellent prices create a dining experience to remember. We've been voted the best again and again in The Georgia Straight, Westender, Where Magazine, Vancouver magazine, and many more. Come see why we're the best Malaysian restaurant in Vancouver!

Ingredients:
½ C. flour
¼ C. rice flour
1 tsp. baking powder
¼ tsp. salt
1 C. water
1 egg, beaten
oil for deep frying
6 ripe bananas, peeled
and cut in two pieces

Instructions:
1. Mix the flour, rice flour, baking powder and salt well in a bowl. Beat the water and egg into the flour mixture until batter is smooth. Set batter aside to rest for anywhere from 15 minutes to an hour.

2. Heat the oil in a deep skillet or deep fryer to between 350° and 375°. Working in batches, using a fork to dip pieces of banana in batter to cover. Let any excess batter drip off and drop in the hot oil to deep fry, turning until well browned on all sides.

3. Drain on paper towels and serve warm.

820 W BROADWAY, VANCOUVER, BC

BANANA LEAF

"The food that enters the mind must be watched as closely as the food that enters the body."
Patrick Buchanan

STIR-FRIED STICKY RICE CAKE

Hidden on the edge of Chinatown, Bao Bei may be hard to find if you aren't looking for it. But that's what makes this Chinese Brasserie an even greater treasure, you are rewarded for your search. If you just keep your ears open, "Bao Bei" is sure to be a recommendation from any regular Vancouver bar and lounge-goer. Bao Bei is Mandarin for "precious," or "darling" and is a term well-suited to the establishment that Owner Tannis Ling and Chef Joël Watanabe have created. Rich with an antique feel, walking into Bao Bei is like being welcomed into an old family home full of quirky antiques and personal touches.

Ingredients:
200g dried sticky rice cake*
90g pork loin
4 tbsp. (60 ml) light soy, divided
3½ tsp. (20 ml) sesame oil, divided
1 tbsp. (20 ml) granulated sugar, divided
50g dried wood ear mushroom strips**
100g bamboo shoots
2 tbsp. (30 ml) vegetable oil
1 tbsp. (20 ml) garlic, minced
2 tbsp. (30 ml) salted mustard greens***, finely chopped
1½ C. (380 ml) chicken stock
1 green onion, to garnish (optional)

Instructions:
1. Rehydrate dried rice cake in water overnight in refrigerator.
2. Julienne pork loin and marinade for ½ hour to overnight in 2 tablespoons (30 ml) light soy, 1½ teaspoons (7 ml) sesame oil, and 1 teaspoon (5 ml) sugar.
3. Rehydrate wood ear mushroom by letting sit in boiled water until tender, about 5 minutes. Drain and set aside.
4. Slice bamboo shoots into ¼-inch (0.5 cm) pieces on the bias and set aside.
5. Heat wok over high heat until smoking; swirl in oil. Add julienned pork and sauté until browned and almost cooked through. Quickly add garlic, mustard greens, wood ear mushroom, bamboo, remaining 2 tablespoons (30 ml) light soy, 2 teaspoons (10 ml) sesame oil and 2 teaspoons (10 ml) sugar. Sauté 15 seconds, not allowing garlic to burn. Add sticky rice cake and chicken stock. Cook stirring vigorously until stock has evaporated to saucy consistency.
6. Serve with finely chopped green onion and sunny-side up egg if desired.

* Found in Chinese supermarkets in 400 g bags and is sometimes called 'rice pasta.'
** Found in Chinese supermarkets either whole or in strips. Mushroom is black on one side and tan on other with velvet skin.
*** Found at T & T in refrigerated section by kimchi.

163 KEEFER STREET, VANCOUVER, BC

BAO BEI

"Destiny cuts the cake of love, three slices to some, to others, a crumb."
Stefano Benni

baru

con alma

2535
OPEN
EVERYDAY

Signature Tastes of VANCOUVER

Latin driven cuisine is the focus of this award winning, Point Grey / Kitsilano neighbourhood restaurant. Here, responsibly caught seafood and local ingredients are served with classic and original drinks...

Ingredients:
1 C. all-purpose flour
salt and freshly ground black pepper
2 eggs
⅓ C. milk
2 C. finely ground cracker crumbs or bread crumbs
1½ lbs. sole fillets
¼ C. vegetable oil (more if needed)

Red Chile Garlic Salsa:
½ C. dried whole red chiles (chiles de arbol)
¾ C. boiling water
¼ C. chopped onion
5 cloves garlic
1 tbsp. coarsely chopped cilantro
1½ tsp. paprika
1½ tsp. ground cayenne
1½ tsp. dried red pepper flakes
½ tsp. chili powder
½ tsp. salt
½ tsp. lemon juice
½ tsp. ground cumin

Instructions:
1. For the salsa, put the whole chiles in a dry, heavy skillet over high heat. When hot, shake the pan so the chiles heat evenly; they should be about half blackened.
2. Immediately put the chiles in a bowl, pour the boiling water over them, and set aside until lukewarm.
3. Put the chiles and their soaking water in a food processor with the onion, garlic, cilantro, paprika, cayenne, red pepper flakes, chili powder, salt, lemon juice, and cumin. Process until well mixed but still slightly chunky. Set aside.
4. Put the flour in a large, shallow dish and season generously with salt and pepper.
5. Beat the eggs with the milk in a shallow bowl. Put the cracker crumbs in another large, shallow dish.
6. Dip a sole fillet in the flour, patting to remove the excess. Then dip it into the egg mixture to coat.
7. Finally, thoroughly dredge the fillet in the cracker crumbs, patting to remove the excess. Set aside on a plate lightly dusted with flour and repeat with the remaining fillets.
8. Heat the oil in a large, heavy skillet over medium heat. Add the sole fillets and cook until golden brown, about 2 minutes.
9. Turn the fish, then drizzle about 1 teaspoon of the salsa over each fillet.
10. Continue cooking until the sole is just cooked through, about 2 minutes longer, depending on the thickness of the fillets.
11. Transfer the sole to individual plates, passing the extra salsa separately. Serve immediately.

2535 ALMA STREET, VANCOUVER, BC

BARU LATINO

"News is like food: it is the cooking and serving that makes it acceptable, not the material itself."
Rose McCaulay

Wild B.C. Salmon with Honey Pepper Glaze on Organic Basmati Rice

Signature Tastes of VANCOUVER

Ingredients:
salmon 140 g
honey pepper sauce
(Yield approx ¾ litre)
125 mls. honey
125 mls. soy sauce, light.
¼ C. golden sugar
250 mls. pineapple juice
60 mls. lemon juice
30 mls. vinegar
10 mls. olive oil
1½ g black pepper, ground
¼ tsp. cayenne pepper
1 tsp. paprika
1 tsp. fresh garlic, minced.
1 C. fresh red, green and yellow peppers, julienne (blanched) 30 g
fresh green onions, sliced
½ C. of water and 3 tbsp. starch
organic brown basmati rice (lundberg)
Note: water to organic brown basmati rice ratio, 1 part rice to 1.75 parts of water
seasonal vegetables

Instructions:

Salmon:
1. Preheat oven to 425F.
2. Set salmon (140 gr.) fillets (skins down) in pan, leaving enough space between them so they can easily be lifted out. Brush lightly with Olive Oil and place in oven.
3. Bake for 10 to 15 minutes or until salmon is just cooked through. Lift the fillets out and set on plate.
4. Spoon Honey Pepper sauce over top sprinkle with julienne of peppers.

Honey Pepper Sauce:
1. Combine in medium size sauce pot – honey, soy sauce, pineapple, lemon juice and olive oil.
2. Bring to boil, add grounded black pepper, cayenne pepper, garlic and paprika.
3. Lightly thicken with starch mixture. Add vinegar.
4. Bring to boil and simmer for 15 minutes, reduce to a syrup consistency. Stirring occasionally. Do not strain.
5. Add blanched peppers and sliced green onions to sauce.

Organic Brown Basmati Rice:
1. Measure out correct amount of rice and place in cooking pot.
2. Measure out correct amount of water and add to rice.
3. Stir well place in rice cooker or pot and cook for 40 minutes or until done.
Note: Organic Brown Basmati Rice is to be prepared just past al dente stage.

Seasonal Vegetables:
1. Steam vegetables and add to plate.

6750 KEITH RD WEST, VANCOUVER, BC

BC FERRIES

"There are some achievements which are never done in the presence of those who hear of them. Catching salmon is one, and working all night is another."
Anthony Trollope

Kiwi on the Green Cocktail

The arrestingly chic design of 300-seat beyond is a marriage of the imagination of the Lorie Lisogar, Owner, Sergio Cocchia, Executive Manager and he inspired au courant magic of Doris Hager of Hager Design & Associates. Beyond is tactile; it's textures, moods and tones grouped as intimate gathering places. It is layers of coulour and contrast. It is muit-leveled, with each area and tier having its own distinct persona.

Ingredients:
1 oz. bacardi white
1 oz. giffard mango tropic
½ oz. aloe
2 oz. kiwi puree
2 oz. fresh lime

Instructions:
1. Shake, strain into chilled martini glass.

2. Garnish fresh kiwi wheel.

BEYOND RESTAURANT AND LOUNGE
1015 BURRARD STREET, VANCOUVER, BC

"Cocktail music is accepted as audible wallpaper."
Alistair Cooke

WHOLE SPOT PRAWNS WITH A GARLIC PARSLEY BUTTER SAUCE

The fare at Bishop's is regional and seasonal. In restaurateur John Bishop's view, it makes sense to showcase British Columbia's lush bounty of seafood, organic produce and meats. His exquisite West Side restaurant blends classic and modern flavours with a casual elegance that keeps clients coming... back for a truly exceptional dining experience.

Ingredients:
1 lb. (500 grams) whole spot prawns, heads on
2 tbsp. (30 mL) butter
2 cloves garlic minced
1 tbsp. (15 mL) chopped parsley
¼ C. (60 mL) dry white wine
salt and pepper to taste

Instructions:

1. Heat a large fry pan on medium high heat. Add butter, garlic and parsley and lightly fry together for 1-2 minutes.

2. Add whole prawns and white wine. Toss together and lightly season with salt and pepper.

3. Cover and cook for 4-5 minutes.

4. Serve in warm bowls with lemon slices and warm crunchy baguette.

2183 WEST 4TH AVENUE, VANCOUVER, BC

BISHOP'S

"It is not necessary to advertise food to hungry people, fuel to cold people, or houses to the homeless."
John Kenneth Galbraith

"Deep Freeze"
(Lavender Honey Nougatine Glace)

Bistro 101 at Pacific Institute of Culinary Arts was founded to create a 'real-world' training experience for the school's professional Culinary and Baking & Pastry Arts students. Pacific Institute of Culinary Arts was the first private training facility in Canada with a fine dining restaurant on the premises. To master all aspects of restaurant organization, our Restaurant Instructors guide students through formal guest service (front of house training).

Signature Tastes of VANCOUVER

Ingredients:
Nougatine:
1 C. sugar
¼ C. water
1 C. almond flakes
Italian Meringue
2 C. sugar
⅓ water
2 tbsp. lavender honey
6 egg whites, whipped to soft peaks
crème anglaise
½ C. milk
½ C. cream
6 egg yolks
¼ C. + 1 tbsp. sugar
½ vanilla pod

Other:
1 C. candied fruit, chopped and soaked in kirsch
2½ C. whipped cream

Instructions:
Nougatine:
1. Caramelize sugar and water until golden in colour.
2. Add almonds and stir until toasted. Pour mixture over parchment paper, let cool and then crush. Reserve.

Italian Meringue:
1. Pour sugar, honey, and water into saucepan and bring to a boil. Decrease temperature to 230F/115C (use candy thermometer).
2. In a separate bowl, whip egg whites to form soft peaks. Bring sugar mixture up to 240F/121C, remove from heat and pour into whipped egg whites.
3. Set aside and let cool for 10-15 minutes.

Crème Anglaise:
1. Cream together ¼ cup sugar and egg yolks until pale yellow.
2. In saucepan, combine vanilla pod, milk, cream and 1 tablespoon of sugar, bring to a boil. Infuse for 30 minutes.
3. Pour vanilla milk into egg yolks, whisking continuously.
4. Return to saucepan and cook over medium heat until the sauce coats the back of a wooden spoon.
5. Strain and cook in an ice bath.

To prepare Deep Freeze:
1. Fold together crushed nougatine, italian meringue, crème anglaise, candied fruit and whipped cream.
2. Pour into moulds, containers or cookie cutters placed on a cookie sheet to freeze. Serve when frozen!

1505 West 2nd Avenue, Vancouver, BC

Bistro 101

"Art is the stored honey of the human soul, gathered on wings of misery and travail."
Theodore Dreiser

BEEF TERIYAKI ROLL

For the past six years executive chef Etsuko Needham and her husband Peter have worked passionately together to provide guests with a unique Japanese dining experience. The result is a restaurant that is refreshing and new, a product of their different cultural backgrounds and experiences. With a firm foundation in Japanese culinary tradition and a passion to explore new territory, Etsuko continues to build on Bistro Sakana innovations, such as the use of brown rice in sushi, and unique Japanese fusion dishes with Italian and French influences.

Ingredients:
5 slices sirloin beef
1 carrot (medium size)
10 green beans
5 stalks spring onion
5 chives
5 tbsp. teriyaki sauce (ready mix)
toasted sesame seeds to taste

Instructions:
1. Marinade meat in teriyaki sauce. Set aside for 15 minutes.

2. Cut carrots, green beans and spring onions in julienne slices. Put the beans and green onion to one side. Drop the carrots into boiling water for a few minutes.

3. Take one slice of meat and roll up with carrots, green beans and green onion. Bundle in some chives.

4. Fry in a frying pan until done.

5. Mix remaining teriyaki sauce with a tablespoon of water and bring to boil.

6. Serve roll meat with sauce and sprinkle sesame seeds on top.

BISTRO SAKANA
1123 MAINLAND STREET #101, VANCOUVER, BC

"No one who cooks, cooks alone. Even at her most solitary, a cook in the kitchen is surrounded by generations of cooks past, the advice and menus of cooks present, the wisdom of cookbook writers."
Laurie Colwin

Chocolate Mousse

Since March 2007 Bistrot Bistro has earned a reputation for one of Vancouver's favourite nights out for French food. Owners Valerie and Laurent's combination of classic French food concepts with contemporary style struck the right chord with the exacting tastes of Vancouver diners. Add an unpretentious atmosphere with warm service and their recipe for a successful French restaurant was complete.

Ingredients:
150g of the best quality chocolate you wish to use
8 eggs

Instructions:

1. Melt the chocolate in a blow on hot water called bain marie.

2. Separate the egg yolk from white. Yolk goes in large round bowl.

3. Beat up the egg white slowly first setting 2 for 1 minute and then 4 for 1 minute then top speed until firm. This is trick to get the maximum air into the mixture.

4. Reverse the bowl if they stick you are good if they drop on the floor well you know what you need to do.

5. When the chocolate is melted mix with the egg yolk quickly to not let them cook or you will have a grainy feel in the mousse.

6. Now for the tricky part incorporation of the egg white to the chocolate. You need to be quick without loosing the air trapped in the white.

7. At once put all the white with chocolate, with a flat cooking spoon both hand at the top of the bowl your left hand turn the bowl half way around and the other cut and turn the mixture delicately.

8. Do not mix or you will have a runny soup for dessert. That the biggest trick.

9. Transfer in a clean bowl and let seat in the fridge for 4-5 hours to settle.

Tip #1: Do not use chocolate milk, it will not set properly.

Tip #2: Only exception is a little drop of coffee extract that enhances the chocolate flavor use the best quality if adding this. You thought it was easy with only two ingredients didn't you, well if you fail come and try ours and if you can't reproduce it we will show you the hands movement. Bon Appetit!

Signature Tastes of VANCOUVER

1961 WEST 4TH AVENUE, VANCOUVER, BC

BISTROT BISTRO

"All you need is love. But a little chocolate now and then doesn't hurt.
Charles M. Schulz

QUEEN CHARLOTTE
ISLAND HALIBUT

Signature Tastes of VANCOUVER

An anchor in Vancouver's culinary landscape, Blue Water Cafe is lauded as the City's definitive destination for seafood. Executive Chef Frank Pabst is known for his innovative and brilliantly executed West Coast plates, insisting on using seafood from wild and sustainable harvest. Raw Bar Chef Yoshiya Maruyama is true to the Japanese culinary aesthetic of pure, clean flavours and ample portions that Blue Water Cafe's Raw Bar has long been famous for.

Ingredients:
Garnish:
1 fennel
1 zucchini
2 cooked artichoke heart
2 cloves of garlic, chopped
1 medium onion, sliced thinly
2 handsfull of baby spinach
¼ C. of extra virgin olive oil
2 tbsp. chopped fresh chives

Halibut:
4 (5 oz.) pieces of fresh halibut, skin and bones removed
2 tbsp. olive oil for cooking
sea salt

Sauce:
1 C. of dry white wine
2 shallots, thinly sliced
4 tbsp. of whipping cream
¼ C. of brown butter
4 tbsp. of drained capers
2 tbsp. of chopped parsley
salt, lemon juice

Instructions:
Garnish:
1. Slice fennel, artichokes & zucchini in quarter-inch slices.
2. Heat olive oil in a stainless steel pot to medium temperature. Add onions and garlic, cook until fragrant then add fennel.
3. Season with salt, add ¼ cup of water, cook until water is reduced and fennel is just done.
4. Add zucchini, season again, cook until zucchini is done, add sliced artichokes and baby.
5. Spinach and stir until spinach is wilted.
6. Adjust seasoning and finish with chives.

Sauce:
1. In a small sauce pan reduce white wine with sliced shallots by ⅔.
2. Add whipping cream, bring back to boil and strain. Whisk brown butter into white wine cream and season with salt and lemon juice. Add capers and parsley.

Halibut:
1. Heat a large enough frying pan (or 2 smaller ones) with the olive oil to medium-high temperature.
2. Season halibut portions with salt and carefully place in hot oil.
3. Sear first side for 3-4 minutes until golden brown then turn the fish around and cook for another 3-4 minutes until the fish is cooked to medium.
4. Take out of pan and place on absorbent paper towel.

BLUE WATER CAFE + RAW BAR
1095 HAMILTON STREET, VANCOUVER, BC

"Food is our common ground, a universal experience."
James Beard

THAI STYLED CRAB CAKES

The Boathouse Restaurant specializes in SEAFOOD — world class, fresh seafood, hand selected by our team of chefs with only the highest quality making it onto the plate. The oceans best is complimented with the highest quality steaks — CERTIFIED ANGUS BEEF, premium cuts aged 35 days, then grilled to perfection. Boathouse offers an extensive wine list with the best and largest selection of BC VQA wines, as well as wines from around the world.

Ingredients:
300 g ocean wise dungeness crab, squeezed
200 g cooked ocean wise baby shrimp
22 g chopped cilantro
22 g chopped basil
1 tsp. minced lime zest
90 ml heavy yolk mayonnaise
1 tsp. lemon pepper
1 pinch sea salt
20 g minced shallots
1 tsp. cracked chili pepper
1 sm egg beaten
120 g panko flakes

Instructions:

1. Squeeze the crab and shrimp to remove excess liquid.

2. Combine all ingredients and mix well.

3. Portion into 90 gr balls.

4. Dip crab cakes in egg wash then roll in panko flakes.

5. Heat a small amount of oil in a Teflon pan.

6. Add crab cakes and cook over medium heat until golden brown, flip over and finish in.

7. Oven for approx 5 minutes (350 degrees).

Wine Pairing: Tyee Gewürztraminer — blended for the Boathouse by Howard Soon.

BOATHOUSE RESTAURANT
1795 BEACH AVENUE, VANCOUVER, BC

"A bad review is like baking a cake with all the best ingredients and having someone sit on it."
Danielle Steel

THE RX
(AKA THE PRESCRIPTION)

Boneta's in house renaissance man, Simon has moved from accomplished barman, to bar manager and now he runs the show, ensuring each guest enjoy themselves to the fullest. Recently named as the 2011 Bartender of the Year, Simon is known to create some of the most delectable cocktails in the city but his real passion is throwing a great party.

Ingredients:
¼ oz. maple syrup
¾ oz. fresh lemon juice
2 oz. makers Mark
fresh cracked pepper

Instruction:
1. Shake and double strain into rocks glass with fresh ice.

BONETA RESTAURANT
1 WEST CORDOVA STREET, VANCOUVER, BC

"Food is not about impressing people. It's about making them feel comfortable."
Ina Garten

Vanilla Creme Brulee

Signature Taste of VANCOUVER

Brix Restaurant and Wine Bar was one of the first restaurants in the development of Vancouver's historic Yaletown quarter as a destination for casual fine dining.... Opening in April 1999 in a turn-of-the-century heritage building on Homer Street it quickly became known for its innovative food, an extensive, well priced wine list, and its warm and inviting atmosphere amid the high-beamed ceilings and original exposed-brick walls.

Ingredients:
1 vanilla bean
2 C. heavy cream
2 C. half-and-half
8 large egg yolk
½ C. plus 8 tsps. superfine sugar
½ tsp. kosher salt

Instructions:
1. Prepare the vanilla: Halve the vanilla bean lengthwise and scrape out the seeds with a paring knife. Position a rack in the middle of the oven and preheat to 325 degrees.
2. Infuse the cream: Bring the cream, half-and-half and vanilla seeds and pod to a simmer in a saucepan over medium heat. Reduce the heat to low and simmer to infuse the cream with the vanilla, 10 to 15 minutes. Discard the vanilla pod. Remove the cream mixture from the heat and cool slightly. Meanwhile, bring a kettle of water to a boil.
3. Make the custard.
4. Whisk the egg yolks, ½ cup sugar and the salt in a large bowl until the sugar dissolves and the mixture is pale yellow and thick; it should leave a trail when you lift the whisk. Pour in the cream mixture in a slow, steady stream, whisking constantly. Skim off any foam or bubbles from the surface.
5. Pour into ramekins: Arrange eight 6-ounce ramekins in a roasting pan and divide the custard evenly among them.
6. Bake in a water bath: Pull out the oven rack slightly, place the roasting pan on it and pour enough boiling water into the pan to come halfway up the sides of the ramekins.
7. Bake until the custards are just set in the center, 40 to 45 minutes. Carefully remove the ramekins from the water bath and transfer to the refrigerator. Chill, uncovered, at least 2 hours and up to 1 day.
8. Prepare the topping: About 30 minutes before serving, sprinkle 1 teaspoon sugar over each custard. Tilt the ramekins to evenly distribute the sugar and tap out any excess.
9. Caramelize the sugar: Holding a kitchen torch about three inches away, burn the sugar until it turns a deep amber. Refrigerate the creme brulees just until the crust hardens, 30 minutes to 1 hour, but not longer (the topping may start to soften). Serve cold.

BRIX RESTAURANT & WINE BAR
1138 HOMER STREET, VANCOUVER, BC

"There is no sight on earth more appealing than the sight of a woman making dinner for someone she loves."
Thomas Wolfe

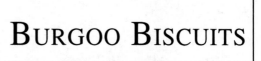

BURGOO BISCUITS

Signature Tastes of VANCOUVER

Burgoo came to life because we believe everyone needs a little comfort and a place to enjoy some great comfort food. No matter what the season is, a tiny bit of comfort can go a long way to making someone's day more satisfying. We felt that creating an old-world, countryside ambience in our locations – through earth tones, natural finishes and materials – would harken back to a simpler time. We hope we've achieved that in some small way and trust that all those who come here experience Burgoo's essence.

Ingredients:
2 C. all-purpose flour
1 tbsp. baking powder
1 tsp. salt
⅓ C. cold butter
1 C. shredded Cheddar cheese
⅔ C. milk
1 egg
½ tsp. garlic powder
2 tsp. dried parsley
½ tsp. garlic salt
2 tbsp. butter, melted

Instructions:
1. Preheat oven to 400 degrees; line baking sheet with parchment paper or grease a baking sheet.

2. Combine flour, baking powder and salt in a large bowl.

3. Cut cold butter into the flour mixture.

4. Add cheese, milk, egg, garlic powder, parsley and garlic salt and mix until combined.

5. Use an ice cream scooper to scoop balls of dough and place them on the prepared baking sheet.

6. Place in the oven and bake for 10 minutes. Brush melted butter over the biscuits and continue to bake for an additional 5 minutes.

7. Remove from the oven and serve warm.

3096 MAIN STREET, VANCOUVER, BC

BURGOO

"Poetry is the synthesis of hyacinths and biscuits."
Carl Sandburg

Sauteed Garlic Prawns

Vancouver's most progressive seafood restaurant. We believe the "c" experience begins with actively sourcing the best local ingredients produced in harmony with our commitment to fostering sustainable farming practice & advocacy. We are devoted to serving you sustainable seafood from our local waters and ingredients that are distinctive and homegrown. As the founding restaurant in the Vancouver Aquarium's Ocean Wise Program, Executive Chef Robert Clark has deconstructed seafood supply lines, dealing directly with the fisherman, to ensure a product that is of the highest quality while respecting environmental sensitivities.

Ingredients:
24 prawns, live and whole
8 oz. (244 grams) of butter, unsalted
4 jalapenos, sliced, seeds removed
8 cloves of garlic, sliced thinly
12 tbsp. (180 mL) of chopped parsley
12 tbsp. (180 mL) of sliced preserved lemon
salt and pepper, to season
8 oz. (240 mL) of backyard vineyards riesling (neck of the woods winery)
microgreens, to garnish
4 tsp. (20 mL) of olive oil

Instructions:
1. In a hot sauté pan, add a little olive oil. Add prawns and butter. Sauté quickly.

2. Add remaining ingredients and deglaze with white wine. Season to taste.

3. Plate and garnish with microgreens.

4. Twist, peel and enjoy.

1600 Howe Street, Vancouver, BC

C Restaurant

"One of the very nicest things about life is the way we must regularly stop whatever it is we are doing and devote our attention to eating."
Luciano Pavarotti and William Wright

61

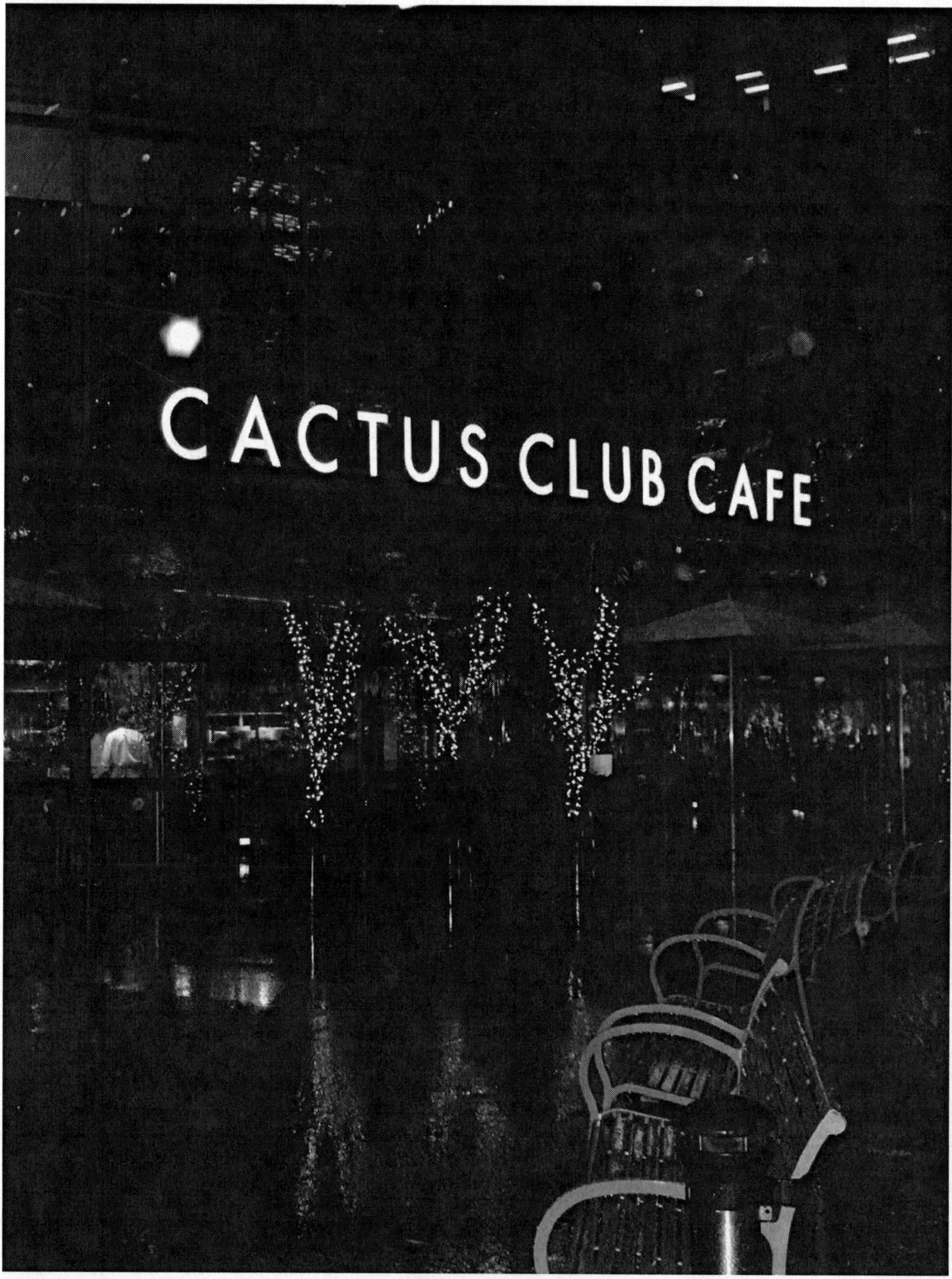
CACTUS CLUB CAFE

Mac 'n Cheese with Lobster

Signature Tastes of VANCOUVER

Ingredients:
Bechamel Sauce:
4 C. milk
2 cloves garlic, peeled and crushed
4 tbsp. unsalted butter
4 tbsp. all-purpose flour
pinch of freshly grated nutmeg
salt and freshly ground white pepper to taste

Mac 'n Cheese:
1 lb. live lobster
2 tsp. vegetable oil
8 oz. Irish or double-smoked bacon, finely diced
4 shallots, peeled and finely chopped
¼ C. grated Emmental
¼ C. crumbled blue cheese
¼ C. grated sharp white cheddar cheese
½ C. freshly grated pecorino Romano
12 oz. dried succhietto pasta, cooked al dente

Instructions:
Bechamel Sauce:
1. Combine milk and garlic in a saucepan on medium heat. Bring to a boil and remove from heat. Cover and leave to infuse for 10 minutes. Strain through a fine-mesh strainer and .discard solids. Make a roux by melting butter in a heavy-bottomed saucepan on medium heat. Whisk in flour and cook for about one minute, or until light brown. Remove from the heat and allow to cool slightly.
2. Add strained hot milk, whisking constantly. Return the saucepan to medium heat and bring the mixture back to a boil, whisking constantly until sauce thickens. Add nutmeg, then season to taste with salt and pepper. Allow to simmer for three more minutes. Remove from heat.

Mac 'n Cheese:
1. Boil large pot of salted water, add lobster. Cook for three minutes at rolling boil. Remove lobster from water, cool. Remove meat, dice the tail and claw meat.
2. Preheat oven to 375 F. Heat vegetable oil in a frying pan on medium heat. Sauté bacon and shallots for about five minutes, or until bacon is just cooked and shallots are translucent.
3. Reheat bechamel sauce on medium-low heat and whisk in Emmental, blue cheese, cheddar and half of the pecorino Romano. Add half of the bacon-shallot mixture and fold in lobster meat.
4. Divide cooked pasta into four individual three-cup casserole dishes and pour sauce over (enough to cover pasta by half an inch).
5. Sprinkle the tops with the remaining pecorino Romano and the remaining bacon-shallot mixture. Bake for 10 to 15 minutes, or until hot and bubbling.
6. Place under broiler for three to five minutes, or until top is light golden brown. Place each casserole dish on a napkin-lined plate.

CACTUS CLUB CAFE
1790 BEACH AVENUE, VANCOUVER, BC

"When I get through tearing a lobster apart, or one of those tender West Coast octopuses, I feel like I had a drink from the fountain of youth."
Joseph Mitchell

Signature Tastes of VANCOUVER

Named after the second holiest city next to Mecca, meaning radiant or enlightened city, this little room is one of the city's most stylish additions. Designed by co-owner Karri Schuermans, Medina was conceived with the purpose of doubling as a high-end private dining room in the evening. Outfitted using green building materials including an exceptional recycled glass bar top and palm wood paneling, Medina has all the makings for a stylish, warm, modern bistro café.

Ingredients:
140 g pork rind
140 g smoked streaky bacon
300 g garlic sausages
600 g dried haricot beans, soaked overnight in 3 times their volume of water
1 celery stick
1 small onion, preferably a white skinned mild one
1 large carrot
6 garlic cloves
2 ripe plum tomatoes
25 g goose fat or 2 tbsp. olive oil
1 bouquet garni
8 pinches of sea salt
2 pinches of freshly ground black pepper
1 clove , lightly crushed
2 tsp. lemon juice

4 confit ducks legs
60 g goose fat or 2 tbsp. olive oil
40 g dried breadcrumbs
1 garlic clove , finely chopped
a handful of fresh flatleaf parsley , coarsely chopped

Instructions:
1. To cut the meats, roll up the pork rind like a Swiss roll. With the seam underneath, use a very sharp knife to cut the roll across into thin slices, then chop the rolled-up slices across into dice. Chop the bacon into small cubes (lardons). Cut the garlic sausage into 1cm thick slices.
2. Drain the soaked beans and discard the soaking water. Tip the beans into a large saucepan, add the diced pork rind and lardons and cover with fresh cold water. Bring to the boil and blanch for 15-20 minutes. Drain the beans, rind and lardons into a colander, and discard the cooking water.
3. Roughly chop the celery, onion and carrot. Peel the garlic cloves but leave them whole. Cut each tomato into eight wedges. (You never see tomatoes in a traditional cassoulet, but chef Raymond Blanc likes them for their colour and sweetness, so he puts a couple in.) Preheat the oven to 120C/fan 100C. (If cooking in a gas oven, use mark 2.)
4. Heat the goose fat or olive oil in a 26cm flameproof casserole or deep overproof sauté pan over a low heat and sweat the celery, onion, carrot and garlic for 5 minutes. Add the tomatoes and bouquet garni and cook slowly to get a sugary caramelisation (about 5 minutes). Add the sausage, beans, pork rind and lardons and pour in 1.2 litres/2 pints water. Bring to the boil, skim off the scum, then add the salt, pepper, clove and lemon juice.
5. Transfer the casserole to the oven and cook, uncovered, for 2 hours, stirring every hour. At the end of this time, the beans will be soft and creamy in texture and the juices should have thickened. You may need to cook it for longer than 2 hours (say up to 2½ hours) to get to this stage - it depends.
6. Remove the cassoulet from the oven. Bury the duck legs in the beans and sprinkle over the goose fat or olive oil, breadcrumbs and garlic. Return to the oven and cook for a further 2 hours. Serve the cassoulet in bowls, sprinkled with chopped parsley.

556 BEATTY STREET, VANCOUVER, BC

CAFÉ MEDINA

"Anybody who believes that the way to a man's heart is through his stomach flunked geography."
Robert Byrne

BASQUE BREAKFAST

Fantastic French Bistro Restaurant in Kitsilano, operated by Steeve Raye, son of Alain Raye, two time Michelin star-winner and operator of the flagship La Régalade French Bistro in West Vancouver. Renowned Chef Alain Raye of La Régalade French Bistro located in West Vancouver, and his son Steeve Raye have opened Café Régalade French Bistro, located in Vancouver's, Kitsilano, March 2011.

Ingredients:
½ link spicy sausage, finely diced (like andouille, chorizo, or linguica)
1 medium sweet onion, diced (walla wallas are fantastic)
2 garlic cloves, minced
2 bell peppers, diced (I like a mix of purple and red, but use whatever you've got on hand)
4 medium tomatoes, diced
1 tsp. fresh thyme (or ½ tsp. dried thyme)
crushed red pepper flakes (to taste)
salt (to taste)
4 eggs (beaten if desired)

1. In a large nonstick saucepan (or skillet with reasonably high sides), saute diced sausage over medium flame till nicely browned, about 4 minutes.
2. Add onion and garlic and stir till well mixed. Cook till onion is soft and garlic is fragrant, about 2 minutes. Add bell peppers and cook a minute or two, till slightly soft. Add diced tomatoes, thyme, red pepper, and salt (if using), cover, and cook 4 minutes, till juicy.
3. If using beaten eggs, stir gently throghout veggie mixture; cover. Cook 4 minutes, till set. (This produces more of a fritatta feel—good for folks who don't like runny egg yolks).
4. If using whole eggs, crack each egg and gently slide it into the veggie stew, trying to keep the eggs from touching each other (it may help to make a well for each egg with the back of a spoon). Cover and cook 3 minutes, till whites are set. Ladle each egg and some veggies into a serving bowl. Serve with crusty warm bread.

CAFÉ RÉGALADE
2836 WEST 4TH AVENUE, VANCOUVER, BC

"A bachelor's life is a fine breakfast, a flat lunch, and a miserable dinner."
Francis Bacon

ENTRECÔTE GRILLÉE

Cafe Salade de Fruits is a casual French cafe dining at best in Vancouver, BC. The main eating area reminds me of a fish and chips restaurant and it's all a bit gimmicky, but it totally works in their favour. The French atmosphere is very played up with a few touristy French memorabilia's like a "no ketchup, no cell phone" sign, newspaper clippings, chalkboards, and photos. Owners Antoine Bonard and Balendran Rameshan run the front end of Cafe Salade de Fruits. They interact with their customers and are both playful characters with a good sense of humour.

Ingredients:
freshly-milled pepper
steak
oil
salt

Instruction:
1. When buying entrecôtes to cook at home, one usually allows a steak of a good ½-inch thickness, weighing 7 to 8 oz., for each person; the steaks should be seasoned with freshly-milled pepper, lightly coated with oil, and grilled, not too near the flame, for about 4 minutes on each side, salt being added as each side is browned. Do not be misled by the name entrecôte minute, often used in connection with these steaks, into thinking that they should be so thin that they are cooked in a minute. It is just a manner of speaking and a thin, flat, entrecôte makes a poor, dry steak.

CAFÉ SALADE DE FRUITS
1551 WEST 7TH AVENUE, VANCOUVER, BC

"Food is a central activity of mankind and one of the single most significant trademarks of a culture."
Mark Kurlansky

campagnolo

Nero
Hendricks gin, Glenfiddich and
Liquore Strega, garnished with
a Cerignola olive

Rob Roy
Glenfiddich, Cinzano red
vermouth, dash of Angostura
bitters garnished with
an orange twist

Pete Marche
Glenfiddich, Orancio vermouth
dash of cherry bitters

CRISPY CECI

Signature Taste of VANCOUVER

Affordable, casual Italian dining in a warm and welcoming space. Campagnolo serves rustic dishes inspired by the Piedmont and Emilia-Romagna regions of Italy in an open, spacious room highlighted by original old growth fir wood beams. Owners and savvy restaurateurs Tom Doughty, Robert Belcham and Tim Pittman of the award winning Fuel Restaurant have created a pleasurable and entertaining dining experience for guests.

Ingredients:
1½ C. dried chickpeas, soaked overnight in water
2 C. baby arugula
1 C. baby spinach
¼ C. fresh mint, torn into small pieces
2 scallions, sliced thin on a bias
¼ C. Italian parsley, leaves sliced thin
1½ tsp. chili flakes
1 lemon, zested and juiced
2 tbsp. extra virgin olive oil
salt
6 C. canola oil

Instructions:
1. Take the soaked chickpeas and cook them in fresh water until very tender. Season with salt at the end of the cooking process. The cooking time (45 to 60 minutes) will vary according to the age of the chickpeas. Once cooked, they can be kept in the fridge for up to two days.
2. In a pot that can hold at least 12 cups (the more the better) bring the canola oil to a temperature of 375F.
3. Drain the chickpeas, dry them on paper towels and then slowly pour them into the hot oil.
4. While they are cooking, add to a large bowl the arugula, spinach, scallion, mint and parsley. After about four minutes of frying, remove the chickpeas and drain well.
5. While they are still very hot, add them to the bowl of greens. Season everything with salt, chilies, lemon zest, juice and, finally, the extra virgin olive oil.
6. Toss very well and check for seasoning. Add more of anything you like, divide among six warm bowls and serve.

1020 MAIN STREET, VANCOUVER, BC

CAMPAGNOLO

"When a man's stomach is full it makes no difference whether he is rich or poor."
Euripides

69

MUSSELS CONGOLAISE

Dim lit supper club with exposed red brick and friendly waitstaff — not to mention excellent food — make Chambar one of Vancouver's most popular restaurants. The meal here ranks up in the top ten. Since Chambar is Belgian and known for their beer selection, some customers decided to pair the courses with beer. It opened their mind as to how beer can be as complex and complementary with food as wine. All of the beers had came at the recommendations of thier waiter who definitely knew the dishes and the beers.

Ingredients:
2 tbsp. olive oil
1½ lbs. mussels (cleaned with a scrub brush under cold water)
¼ red onion, julienned
½ tbsp garlic, minced
½ tbsp ground fennel seed
½ tbsp. ground coriander
½ tbsp. coarse black pepper
½ tbsp. toasted cumin seeds
2 C. coconut milk
1 C. fresh tomatoes, diced
1 tbsp. chipotle purée
½ C. fresh lemon juice
1 C. fresh cilantro leaves
salt and pepper

Instructions:

1. Add olive oil to a 2 or 3-litre pot and heat on medium-high.

2. Add red onions and garlic and allow to cook until translucent (about 2–3 minutes).

3. Add all mussels and immediately add fennel, coriander, cumin and pepper.

4. Add coconut milk, fresh tomatoes, chipotle purée, lemon juice and salt and pepper to taste.

5. Simmer mussels until they have opened. Once opened, add fresh cilantro leaves and serve immediately. Discard any unopened mussels. Makes 2 servings.

562 BEATTY STREET, VANCOUVER, BC

CHAMBAR

"The discovery of a new dish does more for the happiness of the human race than the discovery of a star."
Jean Anthelme Brillat-Savarin

ONION BAJI

Signature Tastes of VANCOUVER

The making of Chutney Villa has been a labor of love. From the constantly reinvented menu, to the carefully chosen decor, to the hit Tamil music that you hear in the background, the Villa has been pieced together from memories, fantasies, and many visits to India. The Executive Chef Ms. Muralee and the sous chef's Mr. Ganesh Shanmugam & Mr. Venkat Srirampillai bring their talent and creativity to the kitchen. With years of experience in the restaurant industry and a passion for cooking, Muralee's natural next step was to open up a restaurant that would introduce Vancouver to the unique flavors of South Indian cuisine.

Ingredients:
2 large onions
3 tbsp.chickpea flour (plain flour will be ok)
1 tsp. garam masala (or to taste)
pinch of chili powder (or to taste)
1 tbsp. mango chutney (the magic ingredient)
vegetable oil for frying

For the Dip:
4 tbsp. plain yogurt
2 tsp. mint sauce straight from the jar

Instructions:
1. Chop onions leaving plenty of longer strands as this improves the final presentation and fry off until soft and sweet. Leave to cool a little.

2. Mix the cooked onions with all the other ingredients except the oil to create a lovely thick paste.

3. Drop dessertspoon fulls into a hot oiled frying pan cooking for a minute or two on each side.

4. Can be taken straight to the table or set aside and reheated in the oven later which works very well.

5. Serve with a yogurt and mint dip—a simple plain yogurt and mint sauce mixture.

"Let first the onion flourish there, Rose among the roots, the maiden-fair Wine scented and poetic soul of the capacious salad bowl."
Robert Stevenson

CIBO'S PAPPARDELLE WITH BRAISED FRASER VALLEY LAMB

Signature Tastes of VANCOUVER

Chef Neil Taylor, of Cibo Trattoria, is transitioning into heavier pasta noodles with heartier sauces for fall. He recently created this pappardelle dish for the fall menu at the restaurant. He uses two flours, a fine and coarse, both available at Cioffi's in Burnaby, La Grotto del Formaggio in Vancouver or in other Italian stores.

Ingredients:
pasta dough
1¼ C. divella farina
Tipo "00" flour
1¼ C. Valli Durum
semolina flour
¼ C. polenta
pinch of salt
4 whole eggs (organic)
4 egg yolks (organic)

Instructions:
1. In a bowl mix the flours, polenta and salt. Make a well in the centre. Add the eggs and egg yolks in the well. Using a fork lightly beat the eggs until smooth.
2. Now start to mix the flour into the eggs little by little until the mixture becomes sticky.
3. Now flour each hand and start to knead the mixture until it becomes smooth and elastic. Wrap in plastic wrap and leave to rest for 30 minutes at room temperature. If preparing a day ahead, refrigerate.
4. Rolling the pappardelle: Roll the dough out with a rolling pin until about 1 cm. thick. With the pasta machine on its thickest setting start to roll out the pasta dough, turning the handle with one hand and supporting the dough with the other hand as it comes through.
5. Now change the setting on the machine by one and roll the dough a bit thinner, dusting the dough with a little flour if needed.
6. Repeat this process until you get to Number 4 on the machine. You should have a long, smooth, shiny, length of dough.
7. Now fold the sheet several times until it is the width of the pasta machine and repeat the process so the dough is rolled in the opposite direction to work the gluten. Start again at the thickest setting and work to about Number 2 or 3 on the machine, or about 1.5 mm thickness.
8. Using a sharp knife, cut the sheets into individual lengths of about 10 inches long by 21z4 inches wide. You now have pappardelle pasta!
9. Dust the pappardelle with a little semolina flour and store on a tray lined with baking paper until needed.

CIBO TRATTORIA

900 SEYMOUR STREET, VANCOUVER, BC

"I don't know what it is about food your mother makes for you, especially when it's something that anyone can make - pancakes, meat loaf, tuna salad - but it carries a certain taste of memory."
Mitch Albom

Grilled Scallops, Roasted Cauliflower, Golden Sultanas and Toasted Almonds

Not cheap but very, very good & one of our all time favorite places for a really special meal. Great West Coast restaurant - upscale without being pompous or formal, so you'll be just as comfortable in jeans or business clothes Very good, eclectic menu, excellent wine list and superb but unobtrusive service - and just as nice in summer.

¼ lb. unsalted butter
12 large sea scallops
(60 g./2 oz., 3 per person)
salt
pepper
1 head cauliflower, cut into small florets
30 g. grape tomatoes (cut in half)
20 g. Italian capers
20 g. slivered almonds, toasted
20 g. golden sultanas, soaked in hot water
100 mL brown butter
15 mL white wine vinegar
10 g. parsley
good finishing olive oil

Optional: 2 chorizo sausages cut into ½ inch rectangles (12 pieces total, 3 pieces per person)

Instructions:

To Brown Butter:

1. Preheat a barbecue, or grill pan to medium-high heat. Melt the butter in a small saucepan. Continue cooking it on medium-high heat until the butter boils and begins to brown. Don't worry if your butter bubbles or foams; just keep cooking it. When the butter begins to brown, you will see specks of darker brown develop at the bottom of the pan. Stir these up and cook until the butter has a nice and even dark honey colour. Remove from heat, strain through a fine sieve and put into a heat-resistant container.

2. Heat a large sauté pan with some olive oil on high heat. Add the cauliflower florets and roast on high heat until they are a golden brown colour. Take out of the pan and set aside.

3. If you choose to add the chorizo, grill on both sides, about 1 minute per side.

4. Season the scallops and give each side cross-hatch grill marks, about 1-2 minutes per side.

5. While the scallops are cooking, re-heat the cauliflower, tomatoes, capers, almonds and sultanas in brown butter. De-glaze the pan with the white wine vinegar; this will become the sauce. Finish with chopped parsley and salt and pepper if needed.

To Serve:

1. Divide the scallops (and chorizo, if so inclined) on the plates and top with cauliflower mixture. Finish with a drizzle of good quality olive oil.

NOTE: Howard suggests pairing the dish with a crisp, fruity wine like La Segreta Bianco from Planeta winery in Sicily, which he recently visited.

CinCin Ristorante + Bar
1154 Robson Street, Vancouver, BC

"I like a cook who smiles out loud when he tastes his own work. Let God worry about your modesty; I want to see your enthusiasm."
Robert Farrar Capon

APPLE AND BERRY PIE

Signature Tastes of VANCOUVER

Occupying one of the busiest corners in the historic Theatre Row section of the Granville entertainment district, Cinema Public House has high-ceilinged foyer that leads two ways – circle-cutout double doors lead to the larger restaurant side while leather-covered paneling conceals the snaking bench and ottomans of the lounge area. The rooms, separated late night by a black velvet curtain, are of a modern design, with subtle hints to the nostalgia of the Theatre Row halcyon days. A large herringbone pattern tile spans the floor, leading to walls finished with black stained and brushed granite oak. 'Octopus' chandeliers by De La Espada light seafoam green chairs of the main dining area, while the bar uses a mirrored drop ceiling and re-purposed desk lamps to achieve the cool, low-light atmosphere that Donnelly Pubs are known for.

6 green Granny Smith apples
100g fresh or frozen mixed berries
50g soft brown sugar
Juice of ½ a lemon
1 small pieces of cinnamon stick
250g short crust pastry

Instructions:

1. Peel, core and dice the apples, Place in pan with sugar, lemon juice and cinnamon stick.

2. Cook until soft, allow to cool. Add the berries. Take ⅓ of the pastry and set aside, take the remaining and roll out with flour into a 8 inch pie pan.

3. Put apple mix in pie pan, roll reminder of pastry for the top. Make a small hole in top of pie, sprinkle with sugar and bake in oven for 20 to 25 minutes until golden.

4. Serve warm with whipped cream.

CINEMA PUBLIC HOUSE
901 GRANVILLE ST., VANCOUVER, BC

"We must have a pie. Stress cannot exist in the presence of a pie."
David Mamet

LINGUINE WITH HALF LOBSTER

Cioppino's Mediterranean Grill & Enoteca are pleased to give you a fresh perspective on Mediterranean cooking with chef/owner Giuseppe "Pino" Posteraro, the 2008 Vancouver Magazine's Chef of the Year, 2009 Restaurant of the Year and gold medal winner at the BC Gold Medal Plates (2007).

Ingredients:

1 L water
100 mL dry white wine
100 g mixed white vegetables (onions, celery, leeks, celeriac)
1 sprig thyme
2 bay leaves
25 g sea salt (about 38 mL)
5 black peppercorns
2 live Nova Scotia lobsters (each 1 kg)
20 mL extra-virgin olive oil
5 mL chopped garlic
1 mL chopped red chili pepper
20 g Roma tomatoes, peeled, seeded and cubed (about 1 tomato)
Splash of dry white wine
75 mL lobster jus (recipe available in cookbook)
80 mL nasty tomato sauce (recipe available in cookbook)
8 g julienned basil (about 30 mL)
10 g chopped Italian parsley (about 35 mL)
30 mL whipping cream
320 g dry linguine

Instructions:

1. In a large stockpot, combine water, the 100 mL of white wine, mixed vegetables, thyme, bay leaves, salt and peppercorns to make a court bouillon. Bring to a boil on high heat.

2. Fill a large roasting pan with ice water. Immerse lobsters, heads first, in the boiling bouillon and cook for 4 minutes. Remove lobsters from the bouillon and immediately plunge them into the ice bath. Once lobsters are cold, split them in half. Leave the tail meat in the shell. Remove the heads (discard the sand sac — the dark sac with a sandy texture, which tastes quite unpleasant), reserving them for another application such as lobster bisque. Extract the meat from the claws and place in a bowl; then extract the meat from the knuckle (very tasty) and place in another bowl. Reserve the shells.

3. Heat olive oil in a frying pan on high heat. Add garlic and chili pepper and cook for 1 minute. Stir in tomato, the splash of white wine, lobster jus and tomato sauce. Season with salt and pepper to taste, then add basil, parsley and cream. Add the meat from the lobster claws, then after 1 minute the tails and the meat from the knuckles. Reduce the heat to low and keep warm. Divide the meat from the claaws evenly among the reserved halved body shells.

4. Bring a large pot of salted water to a boil on high heat. Add linguine and cook for 9 minutes, or until pasta is al dente. Drain well in a colander, then toss with the lobster sauce.

5. To serve, divide pasta, half lobster tails and claw and knuckle meat among four warmed plates. Serve immediately.

CIOPPINO'S MEDITERRANEAN GRILL

1133 HAMILTON STREET, VANCOUVER, BC

"Music with dinner is an insult both to the cook and the violinist."
G.K. Chesterton

Dungeness Crab Cake with Orange Vinaigrette

Coast is where seafood –fresh British Columbia seafood – dazzles! The freshest fish, succulent shellfish and the most colossal seafood towers are here, with the rarest, perfectly prepared oysters nestled in beds of ice, waiting for you. This is BC's best seafood, and offers true west-coast dining, flashy and fun for every mood and every occasion.

Ingredients:
Crab Cake:
3 lbs. picked fresh Dungeness crab meat
3 stalks of celery, washed and finely diced
1 heaping tbsp fresh thyme, chopped
3 C. mayonnaise
2 C. panko breadcrumbs, half reserved for breading
salt to taste

Vinaigrette:
1 egg yolk
1 tsp. Dijon mustard
⅓ C. orange vinegar (white wine vinegar can be substituted)
¼ tsp. orange oil (available at specialty shops)
⅓ C. canola oil
⅓ C. extra virgin olive oil (mixed into the canola)
1 tbsp. honey
salt to taste
cold water to adjust consistency

Instructions:
Crab Cake:
1. Pick through crab meat and discard any shell fragments.
2. Gently squeeze excess moisture from the crab being careful not to break up the leg pieces.
3. Combine all ingredients in a large mixing bowl and mix gently being careful not to overwork the mixture (this will make the cake gluey).
4. Measure out 3 oz scoops of the mixture and form into uniform cakes.
5. Pat the top and bottom of the crab cakes with the reserved panko and refrigerate for at least one hour (may be stored covered in the fridge for 2 days).
6. Extra cakes can be frozen for up to 3 weeks for future use.

Vinaigrette:
1. Combine egg yolk, Dijon, vinegar and honey in a large mixing bowl.
2. Whisk together to combine and add orange oil
3. Gradually add the combined oils while continually whisking (this will create an emulsification or a slightly thickened texture).
4. Taste dressing and adjust flavor with salt as necessary.

Salad and Service:
1. Preheat oven to 425° F.
2. Combine mixed greens with thinly shaved fennel (an inexpensive Japanese mandolin will help with this).
3. Heat an ovenproof pan over med-high heat with canola oil for searing.
4. Sear 1 side of crab cake until golden then flip and place in the preheated oven for 3-5 minutes.
5. Dress the salad with orange vinaigrette and distribute evenly on the plates.
6. Remove crab cake from the oven and plate next to or on the salad.
7. You can garnish the cake with the fennel tops or even a dab of tartar sauce.

Signature Tastes of VANCOUVER

COAST SEAFOOD RESTAURANT
1054 ALBERNI STREET, VANCOUVER, BC

"All the world is birthday cake, so take a piece, but not too much."
George Harrison

Chicken Taquitos

Chefs Stuart Irving and Tyson Reimer along with Jason Kelly, Cobre (meaning "copper" in Spanish) will introduce the Pacific North West to the unique blend of exuberance and sophistication found in Latino food culture. Open the door to Cobre and enter a whole new food experience. Located in historic Gastown, Cobre's interior immediately welcomes you. Warm coppery tones, exposed brick, dark wood, an inviting bar, installation art – you wont find oversized sombreros, non cacti or Pepi Gonzales. This is a kitch free zone.

Ingredients:
1 carrot, cut in small chunks
3 stalks celery, cut in chunks
½ white onion, cut in chunks
1 bay leaf
salt to season
4 free range, boneless skinless chicken breasts
(12) 6" white corn tortilla shells
1 C. corn oil

To Poach Chicken:
1. Bring water to boil with rough cut carrot, celery, onion and bay leaf.
2. Turn down to simmer and add salt to season.
3. Lay in chicken breasts.
4. Poach until just cooked, nice and moist.
5. Set aside to cool.

To Assemble:
1. Heat a small amount of corn oil in fry pan.
2. Quickly blanch tortilla shells.
3. Lightly season with salt.
4. Shred chicken breasts (can use 2 forks to do this).
5. Roll $1/12$ of the chicken in the tortilla shell.
6. Shallow fry until golden brown.
7. Set onto paper towels to drain off oil.

Cobre Restaurant
52 Powell Street, Vancouver, BC

"I don't know which is more discouraging, literature or chickens."
E. B. White

FUME (FISH STOCK)

In the spring of 2010, Cork & Fin discovered a slice of historic Gastown at 221 Carrall St. just off of the entrance to the infamous Blood Alley. Owners Francis Regio and Elliott Hashimoto transformed one of Vancouver's oldest spaces into a haven for those looking for Market Fresh Seafood at an approachable price point. Cork & Fin offers casual dining whether it be on the Raw Bar for fresh shucked oysters, dining on the main level with friends or privacy on the semi-private mezzanine.

Ingredients:

Fume:
equal parts fish scraps and bones
equal parts onion
equal parts celery
1 lemon sliced in half and juiced
pinch salt

Bouillabaisse:
chorizo sausage (meat of one sausage)
1 clove garlic chopped
1 shallot chopped

Instructions:

Fume:
1. Top with water and bring to a simmer (just under boiling) for 2 hours.

Bouillabaisse:
1. Saute and deglaze with 2oz pernod (pastis) and ½ cup white wine.
2. Add half a cup diced tomatoes.
3. Add 2 cups fume (fish stock) and bring to a boil.
4. Add one cobb corn, 8 nugget potatoes, both cut up, 8 mussels, 8 clams, and 8 prawns.
5. Sear small fish fillets.
6. Once mussels and clams have opened pour 1 portion into a bowl. And add seared fish on top.

"Give a man a fish, and you'll feed him for a day. Teach a man to fish, and he'll buy a funny hat. Talk to a hungry man about fish, and you're a consultant."
Scott Adams

BUTTERMILK PANCAKES

Crave on Main, in the trendy and upcoming "Main Street neighbourhood", attracts guests from all locals. The small and intimate interior combines with a lush and charming patio to create an atmosphere that has made this urban delight so widely loved.

Signature Tastes of VANCOUVER

Ingredients:
3 C. all-purpose flour
3 tbsp. white sugar
3 tsp. baking powder
1½ tsp. baking soda
¾ tsp. salt
3 C. buttermilk
½ C. milk
3 eggs
⅓ C. butter, melted

Instructions:
1. In a large bowl, combine flour, sugar, baking powder, baking soda, and salt. In a separate bowl, beat together buttermilk, milk, eggs and melted butter. Keep the two mixtures separate until you are ready to cook.

2. Heat a lightly oiled griddle or frying pan over medium high heat. You can flick water across the surface and if it beads up and sizzles, it's ready!

3. Pour the wet mixture into the dry mixture, using a wooden spoon or fork to blend. Stir until it's just blended together. Do not over stir! Pour or scoop the batter onto the griddle, using approximately ½ cup for each pancake. Brown on both sides and serve hot.

3941 Main Street, Vancouver, BC

CRAVE ON MAIN

"It probably goes without saying that I enjoy the potato pancakes, delicious hams and so forth that maddeningly turn up at this time of year."
Fred Melamed

SWEET POTATO SOUP

Signature Tastes of VANCOUVER

Ingredients:
1 large onion
1 small celeriac
2 carrots
4 sweet potatoes
5 cloves of garlic
1 C. white wine
1 L vegetable or chicken stock, enough to cover the vegetables
¼ lb. unsalted butter
2 tbsp. oil
salt to taste

Bouquet Garni:
4 sprigs of thyme
1 tbsp. coriander seeds
2 tsp. black peppercorns
2 tsp. all-spice
1 tsp. green cardamom
3 cloves
1 tsp. fennel seeds

Instructions:
1. Peel the onion, celeriac, carrots and the sweet potatoes and cut into 1 inch pieces.
2. Heat a large pot with the oil and add in all of the cut vegetables and the garlic, cook for 5 minutes on medium-high heat to achieve a little bit of browning on the bottom of the pot.
3. Sprinkle the vegetables with a generous pinch of salt and then add the white wine and continue to cook until the wine has been absorbed by the vegetables.
4. Add the stock and bring to a boil, then reduce the heat and allow the soup to simmer until the vegetables are tender.
5. Combine all the ingredients for the bouquet garni and wrap them up in cheesecloth and add to the soup while it is simmering.
6. When the vegetables are tender, remove the soup from the heat and allow it to cool for 15 minutes, then puree with the butter in a blender and strain through a fine mesh strainer.
7. Adjust the seasoning of the soup with some salt and serve.

CRU RESTAURANT
1459 WEST BROADWAY, VANCOUVER, BC

"Only the pure in heart can make a good soup."
Ludwig Van Beethoven

FRIED CAJUN CALAMARI

Out of all the restaurants in Coquitlam, we provide an experience closest to upscale Vancouver dining with the most exotic cuisine in town! Our pleasing décor and lighting are suitable for intimate dining by couples, large groups and families. Enjoy live entertainment every Friday and Saturday, in a relaxed environment as our amazingly courteous and helpful waitresses recommend tasty entrees. Sit in one of our comfortable booths at dinnertime and sip a margarita next to our indoor waterfall. We invite you to visit us for a casual lunch or a luxurious dinner to experience our unique atmosphere.

Ingredients:
2 lbs. cleaned calamari (fresh or frozen)
1½ C. unbleached all-purpose flour
¼ C. cumin
¼ C. chili powder
1 tsp. coarsely ground black pepper
½ tsp. salt
2 C. corn oil - more if needed
tabasco sauce, to taste
lemon wedges
cocktail or tartar sauce

Instructions:
1. Rinse the calamari, cut them into ¼-inch rings and place the slices on paper towels to dry. Combine the flour, cumin, chili powder, pepper and salt in a shallow bowl.

2. Heat the oil in a large skillet. When it is very hot, dredge the calamari in the flour mixture, shake off any excess and fry in the oil in batches until light-brown and crispy. As the calamari are frying, sprinkle several dashes of Tabasco on them, depending on how spicy you want them. Drain on paper towels, and serve as desired with cocktail or tartar sauce, with lemon wedges on the side.

Signature Tastes of VANCOUVER

DANIEL'S MEDITERRANEAN TAPAS
2786 BARNET HWY, COQUITLAM, BC

"Food should be enjoyed rather than endured."
Steve Hamilton

THE METROPOLITAN

Diva made its debut at the Metropolitan Hotel in the summer of 1996. Since that time, Diva continues to attract guests both locally and from around the world with its inventive menus of international cuisine firmly rooted in the bounty of the Pacific Northwest. Diva's distinctive setting and playful style reflect the company's entrepreneurial approach to redefining the standard in luxury hotel restaurants. Diva at the Met is a culinary force in its own right and continues to lead dining trends in Vancouver through its unwavering commitment to elevating food into a true art form.

Ingredients:
1.5 oz absolut current
.5 oz. cointreau
1.5 oz. white cranberry juice
fresh seasonal berries
lemon twist

Instructions:
1. First you muddle (mush) the berries in the martini shaker.

2. Then add in the absolute currant vodka and cointreau.

3. Then add the white cranberry juice.

4. Shake then double strain and pour into your chilled martini glass and serve with a lemon twist.

DIVA AT THE MET
645 HOWE STREET, VANCOUVER, BC

"I eat merely to put food out of my mind."
N.F. Simpson

CHILLED SEAFOOD SALAD

The Dockside Restaurant offers superbly prepared classic dishes in a setting like no other. Located on the waterfront where Granville Island faces the city, guests can enjoy panoramic views across False Creek to the world-famous cityscape of Yaletown and beyond to the mountains of the North Shore.

Ingredients:
high quality olive oil
garlic/shallots/Italian parsley/capers
julienne eggplant and roasted red pepper
pinch of chilies
white wine, lemon juice, fish sauce
saltspring island mussels/manila clams
poached tiger prawns, small pieces of pickled octopus
salt and pepper to taste

Instructions:
1. Combine all ingredients except poached prawns and pickled octopus in a large saucepan.

2. Add prawns and octopus towards the end of the cooking process.

3. Sauté until shellfish opens.

4. Separate seafood and sauce, allowing seafood to chill.

5. Further reduce sauce and chill separately from seafood.

6. Pour chilled sauce over seafood and mix in large bowl.

7. Serve chilled with grilled fish: Served with the Dockside Restaurant's Grilled Wild Salmon

DOCKSIDE RESTAURANT
1253 JOHNSTON STREET, VANCOUVER, BC

"The only kind of seafood I trust is the fish stick, a totally featureless fish that doesn't have eyeballs or fins."
Dave Barry

SEAFOOD CREOLE

Looking for some amazing fresh and unique seafood accompanied by an exclusive atmosphere? Dundarave Fish Market, nestled in the heart of Dundarave Village in West Vancouver is just the place! This uniquely characteristic locale showcases some of the most tantalizing fruits of the sea...such as fresh fish and shellfish, delicious crab, shrimp, and halibut cakes, succulent wild salmon, halibut centre cut no skin caught exclusively for the Dundarave Fish Market and so much more!

Ingredients:
1 lb. Digby scallops
½ lb. crab meat
½ lb. shrimp
1 medium onion, chopped
1 C. celery
½ green pepper, sliced thinly
3 tbsp. olive oil
2 cloves garlic, minced
2 tbsp. flour
1 tsp. thyme
1 tsp. basil salt
1 tsp. lemon pepper
1 (540ml) can tomatoes
1 (156ml) can tomato paste
1 tbsp. Worcestershire sauce
¼ tsp. hot pepper sauce

Instructions:
1. Saute onion, celery and green pepper in olive oil and garlic for 5 minutes. Add the flour, thyme, and basil salt to the above, while stirring constantly.

2. Mix together the tomatoes, tomato paste, Worcestershire sauce, and hot pepper sauce.

3. Once mixed, add to the above mixture and simmer for 15 minutes.

4. Add seafood and cook for 3-5 minutes. Serve hot over rice.

DUNDARAVE FISH MARKET
2423 MARINE DRIVE, WEST VANCOUVER, BC

"I'm good in the kitchen. I can cook seafood, collard greens, black-eyed peas."
Monique Coleman

Signature Tastes of VANCOUVER

East is East is a small restaurant located on Main street that caters Indian and vegetarian dishes. The place is actually pretty cool since the restaurant's interior is decorated with an Arabian like theme. Although the tables and chairs are lower compared to the usual height standard of how a chair and table is, these components do add on to the authenticity and vibe of their restaurant theme.

Ingredients:
6 slices bacon
1 tbsp. unsalted butter
½ lb. fresh mushrooms, sliced
3 tbsp. unsalted butter
¼ C. all-purpose flour
1 C. milk
1 (10 oz.) package frozen chopped spinach, thawed and drained
1 tbsp. chopped fresh parsley
2 tbsps. grated Parmesan cheese
salt and pepper to taste
⅔ C. chicken broth
2 eggs
½ C. lemon juice
salt and pepper to taste

Instructions:
1. Separate with wax paper and keep warm until ready to serve.
2. Place bacon in a large, deep skillet. Cook over medium-high heat until evenly brown. Drain, crumble and set aside. Reserve about 1 tablespoon drippings, add 1 tablespoon butter, and saute mushrooms.
3. In a separate saucepan, melt 3 tablespoons butter over medium heat. Whisk in ¼ cup flour, stirring constantly, until a smooth paste is formed. Gradually stir in 1 cup milk, stirring constantly until a smooth thick gravy is formed. Add bacon, mushrooms, spinach, parsley, Parmesan cheese, salt and pepper. Let cook until somewhat thick, about 10 minutes.
4. In saucepan bring broth to a boil. In a small bowl, whisk together eggs and lemon juice. Temper eggs and broth together whisking constantly so as to cook, but not to scramble the eggs. (Cooking eggs to 170 degrees F). Again, salt and pepper to taste.
5. Fill each crepe with spinach and meat filling, roll up, and top with warm egg sauce.
6. Heat the oil in a deep fryer to 185 degrees C/365 degrees F. Dust the prawns lightly with flour. Holding each in turn by the tail, dip them into the batter, then carefully lower them into the hot oil; cook until golden.
7. Fry the remaining prawns and the squid in the same way. Keep warm.
8. Reduce the temperature of the oil to 170 degrees C/ 340 degrees F. Drain the sweet potato and pat dry. Dip the vegetables into the batter and deep fry. Drain well, then keep warm and serve with the dip.

4413 MAIN ST., VANCOUVER, BC

EAST IS EAST

"God comes to the hungry in the form of Food."
M.K. Gandhi

Edible CANADA
AT THE MARKET

Blood Orange Chocolate Cake

Edible Canada (formerly Edible British Columbia) is a six year-old business headquartered at Granville Island Public Market, in Vancouver, British Columbia. We are Canada's largest culinary tourism and locavore retail company, dedicated to sourcing the highest quality culinary products from coast to coast for our customers. Services include our retail & online artisan food store, chef guided Granville Island Market Tours, demonstration guest chef Market Dinners, Gourmet Kayaking Weekends, and popular Amuse Bouche newsletter and blog. In the summer of 2011 we opened Edible Canada at the Market — a vibrant bistro in the heart of Granville Island and at the forefront of Canadian cuisine.

Signature Taste of VANCOUVER

EDIBLE CANADA AT THE MARKET

1596 JOHNSTON STREET, VANCOUVER, BC

Ingredients:
Chocolate Cake:
55ml hot water
224g melted butter, cooled
238ml buttermilk
3 eggs
2 egg yolks
1 tsp. salt
250ml blood orange marmalade
1¾ C. granulated sugar
1 C. all purpose flour
½ C. cocoa
1 tsp. baking powder
2 tsp. baking soda

Dark Chocolate Mousse:
½ C. dark chocolate
100 ml whipping cream

Raspberry Chocolate Semifreddo:
250ml whipping cream
100ml raspberry chocolate sauce
5 egg yolks
50ml sugar

Instructions:
Chocolate Cake:
1. Whisk all the liquids together.
2. Whisk the dry ingredients together and then gradually whisk in the liquids.
3. Spread on a ½ sheet and bake in a 350F oven until springy in the center. Set aside to cool.

Dark Chocolate Mousse:
1. Heat cream until almost reaching the boiling point.
2. Melt chocolate in a bain marie.
3. Add warm milk to chocolate.
4. Beat in mixer until aerated and holding soft peaks.

Raspberry Chocolate Semifreddo:
1. Whip eggs & sugar over a bain marie until mixture holds a ribbon. Whisk in raspberry chocolate sauce, cool to room temperature.
2. Whip cream until cream holds stuff peaks.
3. Fold whipped cream into chocolate mixture.
4. Line a dish with cling film & pour in mixture
5. Freeze for about 2 hrs.

To Plate:
Cut a slice of chocolate cake in the desired size. Top with dark chocolate mousse and serve with a scoop of the semifreddo. Garnish with slices of fresh blood orange, if desired.

"Anything is good if it's made of chocolate."
Jo Brand

STRAWBERRY SOUFFLÉ WITH STRAWBERRY CHAMPAGNE

Chef Dale MacKay and his team at Ensemble have designed a menu that combines classic French techniques, precision execution and unique globally inspired ingredients to create an extraordinary culinary experience in a fun and relaxed environment.

Ingredients:

Soufflé Base:
1 C. strawberry puree
1.5 tbsp. cornstarch
1 tsp. custard powder
1 egg yolk
2 tbsp. sugar

Strawberry Soufflé:
½ tbsp. butter, softened
5 tbsp. sugar
⅔ C. egg whites, room temperature
Soufflé Base

Strawberry Champagne:
1.5 C. strawberries, hulled and roughly chopped
¾ C. strawberry puree
4 tbsp. honey
champagne as desired

Instructions:

Soufflé Base:
1. Place strawberry puree in a large pot over low heat. Simmer until warm, approximately 5 minutes. Keep warm.
2. Place remaining ingredients in a large bowl, whisk to combine.
3. Add ⅓ of heated strawberry puree to mixture in bowl, whisk to combine.
4. To temper yolk, add yolk mixture to pot with remaining puree. Whisk until mixture thickens and comes to a boil, approximately 3-5 minutes.
5. Transfer Soufflé Base into a container, set aside to cool at room temperature for assembly of Strawberry Soufflé.

Strawberry Soufflé:
1. Pre-heat oven to 325F.
2. Grease 6 Le Creuset Stackable Ramekins with butter. Coat with 1T of sugar, removing excess sugar. Place ramekins on a baking tray.
3. Place egg white in a clean dry bowl from a stand mixer and whip.
4. Once egg whites are frothy, add 2.5T of sugar. Continue to whip until egg whites reach a soft peak. Approximately 2 minutes.
5. Add remaining sugar and whip until egg whites reach a medium stiff peak. Be careful not to over whip eggs, to prevent from splitting.
6. Gently fold Soufflé Base into egg whites.
7. Fill ramekins with Strawberry Soufflé mixture. Level mixture with an offset spatula and clean around edges.
8. Place in oven to bake until Strawberry Soufflé rises and is cooked - approximately 9-12 minutes.
9. Serve 'immediately'.

Strawberry Champagne:
1. Place all ingredients, except the Champagne in a bowl. Cover with plastic wrap and place over a pot of simmering water for approximately 20 minutes.
2. Remove from heat, cool in the refrigerator for 15 minutes, strain through a coffee filter into a container.
3. To serve, put desired amount of Champagne into shot glasses. Add Strawberry Champagne mixture to glasses. Serve immediately with Strawberry Soufflé.

ENSEMBLE
850 THURLOW STREET, VANCOUVER, BC

Signature Tastes of VANCOUVER

"One must ask children and birds how cherries and strawberries taste."
Johann Wolfgang von Goethe

GRILLED B.C. SPOT PRAWNS WITH PARMESAN HERB BASTE

Welcome to Finest At Sea Ocean Products Ltd. We are the leading provider of the finest quality seafood on the West Coast. All our products are 100% wild and are caught by our own fishermen through sustainable fishing practices. We have been operating since 1977 as F.A.S. Seafood Producers Ltd. Finest At Sea was established as a 'boutique-style' seafood company here in Victoria and has expanded to several locations in Vancouver.

Signature Tastes of VANCOUVER

Ingredients:
¼ C. freshly grated parmesan or pecorino cheese
2 tbsp. olive oil
2 tbsp. red wine vinegar
1½ tsp. dried basil
1 tsp. coarse-ground black pepper
24 B.C. Spot Prawns, peeled, leaving tail on
12 wooden skewers, soaked in water for 30 minutes prior to grilling

Instructions:

1. In a small bowl, thoroughly blend grated cheese, olive oil, red wine vinegar, basil, and black pepper.

2. Place 2 prawns on each skewer, piercing through both the head and tail sections of each prawn.

3. Transfer to baking tray and brush prawns with baste; cover and refrigerate for 30 minutes. Reserve any remaining baste.

4. Preheat grill or broiler/oven to medium-high heat.

5. Place skewers on a well-oiled grill or spray-coated broiling pan. Grill or broil prawns 5 inches from heat source for 3 to 4 minutes per side.

6. Turn once during cooking; brush with any remaining baste. Cook just until prawns turn pink and are opaque throughout.

1805 MAST TOWER ROAD, VANCOUVER, BC

FINEST AT SEA

"Good food ends with good talk."
Geoffrey Neighor

TOMATO FETA PENNE

Amongst the spectacular gardens and forests of Stanley Park sits the historic Fish House. Relax while we tantalize you with delicious fresh fish and seafood from the Pacific Northwest. Or sit back at the oyster bar with a micro-brewed beer, glass of wine, or a seasonal martini! For a private event we offer three distinctive rooms, 2 which feature patios opening onto the scenic natural beauty of Stanley Park. Whether holding a corporate event, a cocktail reception, family-style dinner or boutique wedding, we will create a memorable experience for you and your guests.

Ingredients:
12 oz. penne pasta
2 tbsp. olive oil
1 L shrimp (uncooked medium, peeled deveined)
3 garlic cloves (minced)
5 plum tomatoes (cut into thin wedges)
6 tbsp. fresh basil (chopped)
3 tbsp. fresh lemon juice
2 tsp. lemon peel (grated)
6 C. spinach leaves (packed baby, ounces)

Instructions:
1. Cook pasta in large pot of boiling salted water until just tender but still firm to bite. Ladle 1 cup pasta cooking liquid into small bowl and reserve. Drain pasta. Return pasta to pot; cover to keep hot.

2. Meanwhile, heat oil in large nonstick skillet over medium-high heat. Sprinkle shrimp with salt and pepper. Add shrimp and garlic to skillet and sauté 2 minutes. Add tomatoes, 4 tablespoons basil, lemon juice and lemon peel and sauté until shrimp are cooked through, about 3 minutes.

3. Add spinach leaves to hot pasta; toss until spinach wilts. Add shrimp mixture and toss to blend. Add enough of reserved pasta cooking liquid to moisten. Season to taste with salt and pepper. Transfer pasta to bowl.

4. Sprinkle with remaining 2 tablespoons basil and serve.

FISH HOUSE IN STANLEY PARK
8901 STANLEY PARK DRIVE, VANCOUVER, BC

"Vegetables are the food of the earth; fruit seems more the food of the heavens."
Sepal Felicivant

Renowned as one of West Vancouver's most celebrated dining experiences , Fraîche is a feast for the senses. The bright and elegant dining room serves as a backdrop for the highly acclaimed menu and as a frame for the panoramic view. Led by rising culinary talent Executive Chef, Jefferson Alvarez, Fraîche offers delicious and diverse menus for lunch, dinner, and brunch that incorporate westcoast sensibilities and ingredients with global flare and flavours.

Signature Tastes of VANCOUVER

Ingredients:
Pastry:
225 g bread flour
110 g of butter
1 pinch of salt
65 ml water
1 egg yolk

Royale (custard base for quiche):
8 eggs
1 L 35% cream
3 lemon zested
1 leek sliced on half, chopped and sautéed
8 g chopped tarragon
3 g of chopped dill
½ C. of BC sweet corn
350 g of lobster

Instructions:
1. Combine the first four pastry ingredients together in the mixer or by hand in a bowl.
2. Knead swiftly in to a dough. Wrap the dough in cling film and let it rest in the fridge overnight.
3. Roll out the pastry to about ⅛" thick and line an 8" tart ring with the dough.
4. Blind bake the shell at 360F for 30 mins. Remove from oven and brush the hot shell with egg yolk.

For the Filing:
1. Mix the eggs and cream with the tarragon and dill, add salt to taste, and after the mix is well incorporated add the rest of the ingredients and pour in to the pastry shell.
2. Cover with foil or parchment paper and bake at 350 F for approximately 35 minutes.
3. The finished quiche should no longer jiggle in the middle.

2240 CHIPPENDALE ROAD, WEST VANCOUVER, BC

FRAÎCHE

"A woman should never be seen eating or drinking, unless it be lobster salad and Champagne, the only true feminine and becoming viands."
Lord Byron

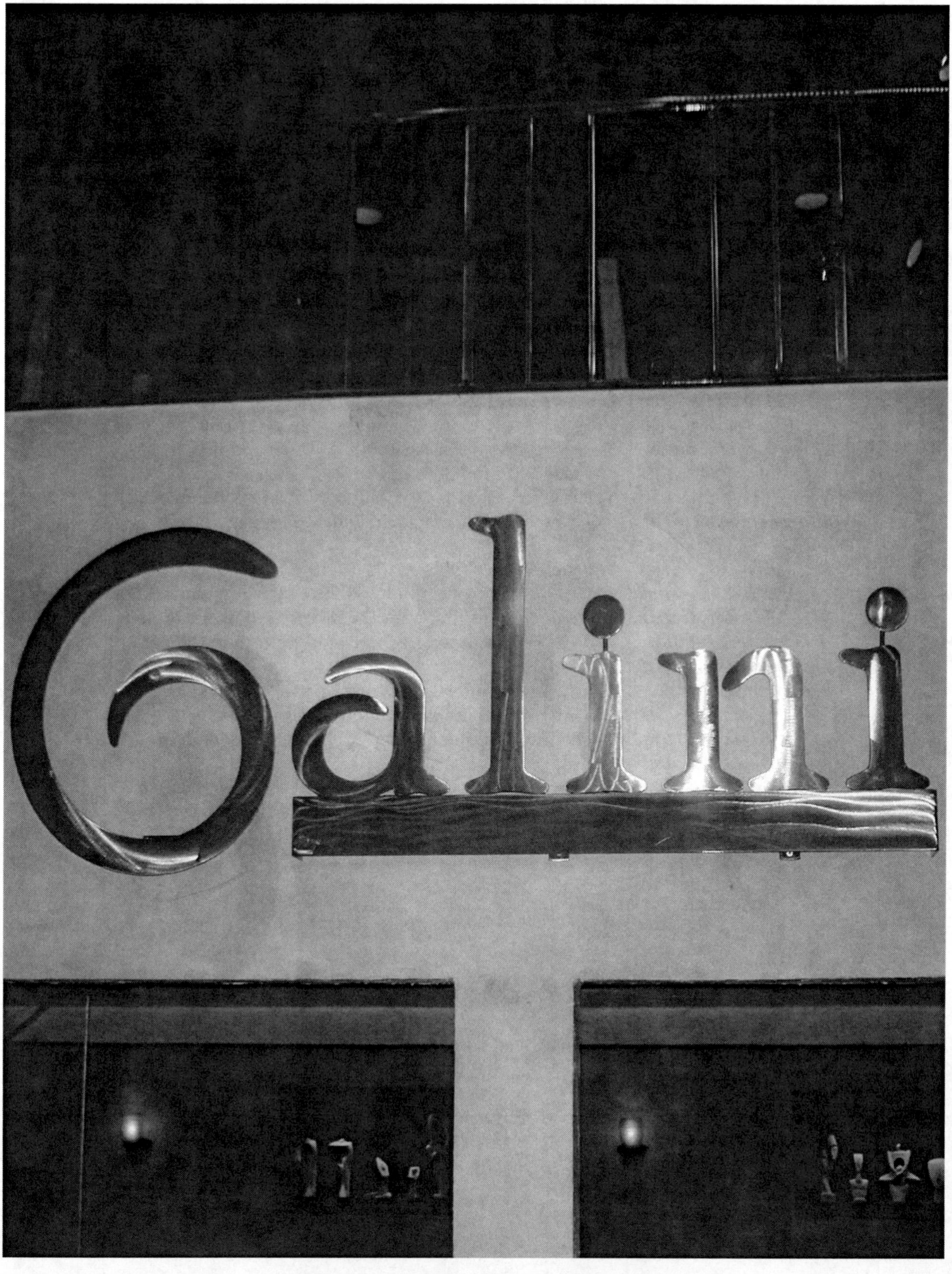
Galini

BACON WRAPPED SCALLOPS

The countryside of Epirus, Greece is rich in olive orchards, eclectic fruit trees, home grown vegetables, fresh cheeses, and homemade yogurt. This is home to both, executive chef John Ikonomou and Angela Ikonomou, whom grew up to appreciate fresh ingredients and the food it produces – setting the foundations for Galini.

Ingredients:
2 lbs. bacon (regular sliced, not thick)
2 lbs. sea scallops (if very large, cut in half)
3 tbsp. butter
1 tbsp. minced garlic
⅓ C. chicken broth

Instructions:

1. Cut bacon strips in half.

2. Wrap a piece of bacon around each scallop; secure with toothpick.

3. Arrange the wrapped scallops on a baking sheet.

4. Broil 5 inches from heat for 3 minutes per side, or until bacon is crisp.

5. In small skillet, melt butter; add garlic and saute 1 minute.

6. Add broth and bring to a boil.

7. Cook 2 minutes.

8. Place scallops in large bowl; pour broth over. Gently toss to coat.

GALINI GREEK KOUZINA & GRILL

19475 FRASER HIGHWAY, SURREY, BC

"Bacon is the candy of meat."
Kevin Taggart

Signature Tastes of VANCOUVER

Giraffe Restaurant is an intimate water front restaurant with a west coast fusion menu located in White Rock, BC Canada. Since 1989 Giraffe has delighted locals as well as diners from West Vancouver to Seattle with it's innovative and creative use of local fresh ingredients including ocean wise seafood.

Ingredients:
8 C. chopped fresh tomatoes
2 tsp. chicken bouillon granules
1¼ tsp. salt
½ tsp. pepper
2 celery ribs, finely chopped
½ C. finely chopped onion
2 garlic cloves, minced
½ tsp. crushed red pepper flakes
6 tbsp. butter, divided
¼ C. all-purpose flour
6 C. milk, divided

Instructions:

1. In a large saucepan, simmer tomatoes, bouillon, salt and pepper for 30 minutes.

2. Meanwhile, in a skillet, saute celery, onion, garlic and pepper flakes in 2 tablespoons butter until tender; add to the tomatoes.

3. In another saucepan, melt the remaining butter; stir in flour until smooth. Gradually add 2 cups milk. Bring to a boil; cook and stir for 2 minutes or until thickened and bubbly. Add tomato mixture. Stir in the remaining milk; heat through (do not boil).

15053 MARINE DRIVE, WHITE ROCK, BC

GIRAFFE

"A first-rate soup is more creative than a second-rate painting."
Abraham Maslow

PAN SEARED
QUEEN CHARLOTTE HALIBUT

This room is a Vancouver icon, and its chameleon qualities are alive with energy day and night. From studious business lunches to early evening dinner, the room morphs and changes as the night wears on. After the plates are cleared the volume goes up and the evening is still very, very young indeed. Steaks. Seafood. A little something. A big deal. It's all things to all people. You haven't been to Vancouver until you've been to Glowbal.

Signature Tastes of VANCOUVER

Ingredients:
Part A:
7 oz Halibut
salt and pepper
1 fl oz of canola oil
1 tsp. of butter

Part B:
1 fl oz of olive oil
¼ C. of green onion
¼ C. of yellow onion
1 tsp. of minced garlic
1 tsp. of sambal oelek
¼ C. of diced tomatoes
1 C. of pre cooked
cannellini beans
½ C. of chicken stock
1 tsp. of unsalted butter
handful of spinach
season to taste

Instructions:
Part A:
1. Preheat an oven to 400 degrees.
2. Heat a frying pan or skillet to medium high heat.
3. Pat your halibut dry with paper towel and season with salt and pepper.
4. Add your canola oil to the pan and carefully place the halibut in the pan.
5. Cook for approximately 3 min. add butter to the pan and place in the oven for 4 min or until cooked – with halibut when you lightly press on the outside of the fish it should feel as if it would flake apart if you were to add more pressure, at this point it is medium to medium well.

Part B:
1. Heat a frying pan to medium heat.
2. Add olive oil, green onions, white onions for 30 seconds or until translucent.
3. Add garlic and sauté for 15 seconds.
4. Add sambal oelek and diced tomatoes.
5. Add the pre cooked beans and stew for 3 to 4 minutes.
6. Add chicken stock and cook until desired consistency.
7. Finish by adding butter and spinach, continue to cook on low heat until butter has melted and the spinach is wilted.

GLOWBAL GRILL & SATAY BAR

1079 MAINLAND STREET, VANCOUVER, BC

"I have a face that is a cross between two pounds of halibut and an explosion in an old clothes closet."
David Niven

AS is young boy grown up in India, Joginder learned to cook while caring for his ailing mother. After spending 16 years with Air Canada as a flight attendant and seeing the world, he chose Maple Ridge as his home. With his wife Swarnjit they serve up the best east Indian & European cuisine around. Over the past 10 years they have received many awards and appeared in the Vancouver Sun & The Province several times. They are also well known for their world famous cheesecakes baked fresh on the premises. Everyone at GM restaurant would like to thank all their friends & customers for helping to make their business such a success.

Ingredients:
2 tbsp. oil or ghee
1 onion, chopped
6 cloves garlic, minced
1 tbsp. gingerroot, minced
2 tsp. coriander, ground
½ tsp. turmeric
¼ to ½ tsp. cayenne pepper (optional)
1 lb. spinach, chopped
1 C. water
1½ tsp. salt
1 C. yogurt
¼ C. cream (optional)

Instructions:

1. Heat the oil or ghee in a large pot or saucepan over medium flame. Add the onions and sauté until translucent. Add the garlic, ginger and spices and sauté for another 2 to 3 minutes.

2. Stir in the spinach, water and salt and bring to a boil. Reduce heat to low and simmer for another 10 to 15 minutes.

3. Remove from heat, allow to cool a bit. Then use a blender or food processor to puree in batches.

4. Return the puree to the pot. Add a little water if necessary and simmer another 5 to 10 minutes.

5. Stir in yogurt and return to brief simmer and immediately remove from heat. Stir in the optional cream, adjust seasoning and serve.

Signature Tastes of VANCOUVER

20726 LOUGHEED HIGHWAY #3, MAPLE RIDGE, BC

GM RESTAURANT

"A house is not a home unless it contains food and fire for the mind as well as the body."
Benjamin Franklin

IN SUPPORT OF LOCAL FISHERMEN

SPRING + SUMMER HOURS:
TUES-FRI: 11:30-6:30
SAT-SUN: 12:00-6:30
IN A HURRY? 604-730-5040
CALL AHEAD!

GRILLED SALMON TACOS

As a seaside city known for its great food, Vancouver is surprisingly short on establishments offering everyone's favourite meal. That meal, of course, is fish and chips. Look no further good cod lovers, for now you can thank Poseidon - not to mention owner Gord Martin of Bin 941/942 fame - for Go Fish. Located at the public fish sales docks near Granville Island, Go Fish prides itself on using locally caught cod, salmon, halibut and various other shellfish, all of which are acquired straight from the fishing boats that catch them in the harbour.

Ingredients
Pickled Onions:
1 red onion, halved, thinly sliced
3 tbsp. unseasoned rice vinegar
3 tbsp. mirin (sweet Japanese rice wine)*

Chipotle Mayonnaise:
1 C. mayonnaise
4 tsp. adobo sauce from canned chipotle chiles in adobo**

Jicama Salad:
2 C. coarsely grated peeled jicama
2 C. thinly sliced green cabbage
¼ C. chopped fresh cilantro
1 tbsp. fresh lime juice
fish
1-lb. skinless salmon fillet
1 tbsp. achiote paste***
1 tbsp. olive oil

Salsa:
1 lb. plum tomatoes, diced
1 C. chopped white onion
¼ C. chopped fresh cilantro
3 tbsp. fresh lime juice
1 serrano chile with seeds, minced
8 flour or corn tortillas
olive oil
chili powder

*Available in the Asian foods section of some supermarkets and at Japanese markets.
**Available at some supermarkets and at specialty foods stores and Latin markets.
***A paste made from achiote seeds; available at Latin markets.

Instructions:
Pickled Onions:
1. Mix all ingredients in medium bowl. Season to taste with salt and pepper. Cover and chill overnight.

Mayonnaise:
1. Mix both ingredients in small bowl; season to taste with salt. Cover; chill overnight.

Jicama Salad:
1. Toss all ingredients in large bowl; season to taste with salt and pepper. Cover; chill 2 hours or overnight.

Fish:
1. Place fish on plate. Mix achiote paste and oil in another small bowl to blend; rub over both sides of salmon. Cover and chill 4 hours.

Salsa:
1. Mix first 5 ingredients in another medium bowl. Season salsa to taste with salt and pepper. Let stand 1 to 2 hours to allow flavors to blend.
2. Prepare barbecue (medium-high heat). Grill salmon until just opaque in center, about 4 minutes per side. Transfer salmon to plate; let rest 5 minutes.
3. Brush tortillas with oil; sprinkle with chili powder.
4. Grill tortillas 30 seconds per side to heat through.
5. Cut salmon into chunks; transfer to platter. Serve fish with pickled onions, chipotle mayonnaise, jicama salad, salsa, and tortillas.

GO FISH OCEAN EMPORIUM
1505 W 1ST AVE, VANCOUVER, BC

"The race was fun, but the fish tacos and the beer garden helped, too. It was that kind of race. Just fun."
Chris Phillips

WILD MUSHROOM RISOTTO

Signature Tastes of VANCOUVER

The Gourmet Warehouse was founded by Caren McSherry in 1998 to serve the growing market for high quality gourmet foods and supplies in Vancouver. Originally in a warehouse space on Pandora Street, we've since grown and moved to a larger storefront on East Hastings, at Clark and Hastings, and we're open everyday. The Gourmet Warehouse offers thousands of select import gourmet items, specialty housewares, gadgets and tools for the professional or serious amateur cook. We pride ourselves in our knowledge, service and high energy performance.

Ingredients:
½ *medium yellow onion, diced fine*
3 *tbsp. unsalted butter*
1½ *C. Arborio rice, preferably a superfino brand*
½ *C. dry white wine*
5-6 *C. chicken or vegetable or beef stock (keep it hot in the pot)*
½ *C. dry wild mushrooms, soaked in 2 C. of hot water, squeezed of most of their liquid and chopped*
½ *C. freshly grated parmesan cheese*
2 *tbsp. unsalted butter drizzle of truflle oil, (optional)*

Instructions:
1. Place the onion and the butter in a heavy bottomed pot, with the heat on medium cook until it is soft but not brown.
2. Add the rice to the pot and cook until it becomes translucent, this will take about 3-5 minutes. Once the rice is translucent, add the wine all at once. Stir the rice until the wine is absorbed.
3. Begin adding the hot chicken stock a cup at a time, stirring all the while. Continue to stir the rice until the stock is absorbed. Once the stock is absorbed, add another cup and proceed to stir in the same manner until the stock is absorbed again. When you are about ½ way through the stock, add in the chopped mushrooms. Continue with adding the stock and stirring until the rice is cooked to your liking. It should be cooked al dente, still firm but not mushy.
4. To finish the dish, season with sea salt, freshly ground pepper, the remaining butter and parmesan cheese.
5. Just before serving the risotto, lightly drizzle truffle oil over the top, it makes this dish truly heavenly.

GOURMET WAREHOUSE
1340 EAST HASTINGS STREET, VANCOUVER, BC

"Life is too short to stuff a mushroom."
Shirley Conran

GRANVILLE ISLAND BEER BREAD

In 1984 something happened that forever changed the local beer industry: Granville Island Brewing opened the doors to Canada's first microbrewery. In doing so, we opened hearts and minds to a whole new beer drinking experience. Over the years, we've become more than just the local brewery. We focus much of our sustainability efforts towards ongoing community investment, including sponsorship and charitable support, involvement with local sports teams, community organizations and more. We're just as proud of that as we are about what we put in our bottles.

GRANVILLE ISLAND BREWERY
1441 CARTWRIGHT STREET, VANCOUVER, BC

Signature Taste of VANCOUVER

Ingredients
Night Before:
1¼ C. bread flour
¾ C. tepid water
¼ tsp. instant yeast

Day of:
1 - 12 oz Granville Island beer (room temperature)
¼ C. olive oil
3 tbsp. dried onion flakes
4 tsp. instant yeast
½ tsp. ground pepper
¼ C. sugar
4 - 4½ C. bread flour
1½ C. farmers sausage
2 - 3 C. grated Monterey Jack cheese

Instructions:
1. The night before, combine 1¼ bread flour, ¾ cup tepid water and ¼ teaspoon instant yeast, cover with plastic wrap and set aside until next day.
2. The next morning, pour the night before mixture into a large bowl. Add in the room temp. bottle of beer, olive oil, dried onion flakes, 1 cup of bread flour, instant yeast, salt, pepper and sugar, with a wooden spoon mix all these ingredients together until well blended.
3. Mix in another 1½ cups of flour. Sprinkle some more flour onto a flat surface. Pour out the wet dough onto the floured surface, place a little more flour on top.
4. Start to knead the dough and continue to add a little flour till the dough becomes smooth (a little on the tacky side). Knead the dough for about 8 minutes, then place into a lightly oiled bowl, turn the dough over so all the sides are lightly coated. Cover with plastic and let rise for 1 hour or till it has doubled in size.
5. Sprinkle a little flour onto a flat surface and pour out the dough. Add the farmers sausage or any other cooked sausage you like.
6. Add 1 cup of cheese and knead till all incorporated. Cover dough with plastic wrap and allow to rest for another 15 minutes.
7. Afterwards cut dough in half, shape into loaves and place onto a cornmeal parchment lined cookie sheet. Cover with plastic wrap and allow to rest for 1 hour.
8. Using a sharp knife score the dough about an inch deep. Sprinkle the rest of the grated cheese on top of the loaves. Bake in a preheated 350F oven for 30-35 minutes or until a thermometer placed into middle of loaf reads 180F-190F. Remove from oven and allow to cool on a wire rack.

"Beer, it's the best damn drink in the world."
Jack Nicholson

Balsamic and Honey Braised Lamb Shank

The Donnelly Group's flagship cocktail tavern was reimagined in 2011, with a well-appointed and casually elegant design. The venue's expansive back bar is over 9 feet high and constructed of red oak, well-stocked with the makings for the cocktails that inform the rooms drink selection. Antique seltzer bottles, classic novels and assorted oddities sit behind glass while the smooth black bartop is dimly lit by limited edition Art Deco-inspired pendant lamps. The Granville Room' menus are focused on cocktail and beer selections guaranteed to pique the interest of experienced imbibers and novices alike, paired with a boutique dining menu to match the rooms contemporary classic feel.

Ingredients:
4 (1 lb) lamb shanks
4 tbsp. extra virgin olive oil
1 C. honey
½ C. balsamic vinegar
4 C. veal stock

Yam and Parsnip Mash:
2 lbs. yams
1 lb. parsnips
2 tbsp. unsalted butter
1 tbsp. extra virgin olive oil

Instructions:
Lamb:
1. Pre heat oven to 425F. Season lamb shank with salt and freshly ground black pepper.
2. Heat oil in a large roasting pan.
3. Add the lamb shanks and cook until brown all over, about 15 min. Pour the balsamic vinegar and honey over the lamb shanks, add the veal stock and stir to loosen bits from the pan.
4. Bring to a boil, cover with a lid and transfer the pan to the oven. Braise until the meat is fork tender; about 2½ hours.

Yam and Parsnip Mash:
1. Peel the yams and parsnips then place in a large saucepan, cover with water, and bring to a boil over high heat.
2. Lower heat and simmer until vegetables are fork tender, about 10 to 15 minutes.
3. Drain vegetables and return to pan. Add the butter and olive oil.
4. Mash until evenly combined and season with salt and freshly ground black pepper.

957 GRANVILLE STREET, VANCOUVER, BC

GRANVILLE ROOM

"The way you cut your meat reflects the way you live."
Confucius

SUN-DRIED TOMATO BREAD DIP

This vibrant Pacific Northwest brasserie, annually recognized by western Canada's pre-eminent food publications and their reader's as one of the 'best hotel' restaurants, continues to excite! Griffins gorgeous sun-washed interior, complete with high-arching windows, features a unique open kitchen concept.

Signature Tastes of VANCOUVER

Ingredients:
12 dry sun-dried tomatoes
½ chopped onion
2 C. extra virgin olive oil
1 C. balsamic vinegar
1 clove crushed garlic
2 tbsp. freshly chopped basil
1 medium diced hot pepper

Instructions:

1. Blanch the sun-dried tomatoes in boiling water for 3 minutes.

2. Remove from water and chop.

3. In a saucepan simmer the onions, (blanched) sun-dried tomatoes, garlic in 1 cup of olive oil for 30 minutes.

4. Pour into a blender with the hot pepper and basil, blend for 7 seconds.

5. Add balsamic vinegar and remaining oil.

6. Refrigerate for 6 hours. Place into a sealed container. This bread dip will last for 2 weeks in the fridge.

900 WEST GEORGIA STREET, VANCOUVER, BC

GRIFFINS

"Sleep 'til you're hungry, eat 'til you're sleepy.
Anonymous

GRUB
MOUSTACHE
MASTERS
SERIES
604.876.8671
www.grubonmain.ca

At Grub it is our expressed desire to nourish and quench with our smaller fixed menu as well as our ever-chanigng daily fresh sheet that reflects the seasons bounty, as well as our own personal whimsy. Sip on a fine gin cocktail, or perhaps indulge in a punch party... good tunes and good times. We look forward to seeing you all soon.

Ingredients:
6 slices bacon
1 tbsp. unsalted butter
½ lb. fresh mushrooms, sliced
3 tbsp. unsalted butter
¼ C. all-purpose flour
1 C. milk
1 (10 oz.) package frozen chopped spinach, thawed and drained
1 tbsp. chopped fresh parsley
2 tbsp. grated Parmesan cheese
salt and pepper to taste
⅔ C. chicken broth
2 eggs
½ C. lemon juice
salt and pepper to taste

Instructions:
1. Prepare Basic Crepes recipe according to recipe directions. Separate with wax paper and keep warm until ready to serve.
2. Place bacon in a large, deep skillet. Cook over medium-high heat until evenly brown. Drain, crumble and set aside. Reserve about 1 tablespoon drippings, add 1 tablespoon butter, and saute mushrooms.
3. In a separate saucepan, melt 3 tablespoons butter over medium heat. Whisk in ¼ cup flour, stirring constantly, until a smooth paste is formed. Gradually stir in 1 cup milk, stirring constantly until a smooth thick gravy is formed. Add bacon, mushrooms, spinach, parsley, Parmesan cheese, salt and pepper. Let cook until somewhat thick, about 10 minutes.
4. In saucepan bring broth to a boil. In a small bowl, whisk together, eggs and lemon juice. Temper eggs and broth together whisking constantly so as to cook, but not to scramble the eggs. (Cooking eggs to 170 degrees F). Again, salt and pepper to taste.
5. Fill each crepe with spinach and meat filling, roll up, and top with warm egg sauce.
6. Heat the oil in a deep fryer to 185 degrees C/365 degrees F. Dust the prawns lightly with flour. Holding each in turn by the tail, dip them into the batter, then carefully lower them into the hot oil; cook until golden.
7. Fry the remaining prawns and the squid in the same way. Keep warm.
8. Reduce the temperature of tile oil to 170 degrees C / 340 degrees F. Drain the sweet potato and pat dry. Dip the vegetables into the batter and deep fry. Drain well, then keep warm and serve with the dip.

"Eating without conversation is only stoking."
Marcelene Cox

北口家 Guu

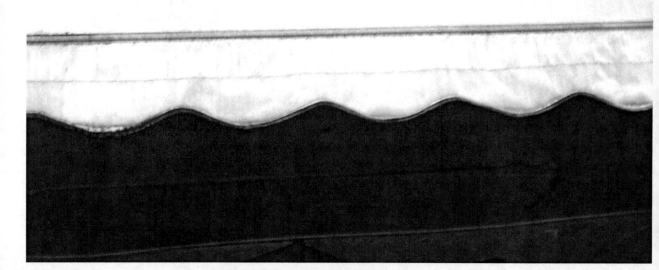

今日もいちにち お疲れさま。

PORK-TENDERLOIN CUTLET

This very first Izakaya was established in 1993, and changed its name to "Guu" in 2000. Guu keeps its pride as the original and offers the most authentic izakaya dish with quick and affordable prices.

Signature Taste of VANCOUVER

Ingredients:
1 lb. pork tenderloin (trimmed)
¾ tsp. salt
¼ tsp. black pepper (fresh coarse ground)
½ C. plum (jam, preserves)
1 tbsp. brown sugar
1 tbsp. peeled fresh ginger (grated)
2 cloves cloves garlic (crushed with garlic press)
1 tbsp. fresh lemon juice
½ tsp. ground cinnamon
4 plums (pitted and cut in half 1 pound)

Instructions:
1. Prepare grill.
2. Using sharp knife, cut tenderloin lengthwise almost in half, being careful not to cut all the way through.
3. Open and spread flat like a book.
4. With meat mallet or between two sheets of plastic wrap or waxed paper with rolling pin, pound meat to ¼-inch thickness.
5. Cut crosswise into 4 equal pieces; sprinkle cutlets with salt and pepper.
6. In small bowl, combine plum jam, brown sugar, ginger, garlic, lemon juice, and cinnamon.
7. Brush one side of each cutlet and cut side of each plum half with plum glaze.
8. Place cutlets and plums on grill over medium heat, glaze side down, and cook 3 minutes.
9. Brush cutlets and plums with remaining plum glaze; turn pork and plums over and cook until cutlets are lightly browned on both sides, just after lose their pink color throughout, and plums are hot, about 3 minutes longer.

838 THURLOW STREET, VANCOUVER, BC

GUU ORIGINAL

"I'm carrying so much pork, I'm beginning to get trichinosis."
Phil Gramm

SPOT PRAWN COBB SALAD

The Hamilton Street Grill is a contemporary steakhouse featuring Certified Angus Beef along with a large selection of fresh seafood entrees. If it is something a little lighter you are looking for; there is a large Tapas style menu that is sure to fit the bill. The atmosphere is warm and inviting and you're sure to feel comfortable whether seated at one of the nicely spaced tables or in one of the cozy booths. The large patio is heated and great for people watching. You'll want to remember, being open late this is a great spot for dessert after events as well as dinner or appetizers before. Remember to ask about the private room for your next party or business meeting.

Ingredients:

Dijon Mustard Vinaigrette:
2 tbsp. white wine vinegar
1 tbsp. and 1½ tsp. grainy Dijon mustard
1½ tsp. smooth Dijon mustard
1 tbsp. honey
½ tsp. salt
⅓ C. canola oil
⅓ C. olive oil

Cobb Salad:
3 spot prawns, shells on but heads removed
½ avocado
3 C. organic mixed salad greens, chilled
2 tbsp. Dijon mustard vinaigrette
2 oz. Poplar Grove Tiger Blue cheese or your favourite, room temperature, crumbled
1 large heirloom tomato, in ¼-inch dice or 12 teardrop or grape tomatoes
2 large eggs, hard-boiled and peeled, in ¼-inch slices
4 slices bacon or pancetta, diced and cooked until crisp

Instructions:

Vinaigrette:
1. Combine vinegar, mustards, honey and salt in food processor or blender at high speed for 30 seconds. With motor running, slowly add canola and olive oils in steady stream, then process for another 30 seconds. Refrigerate until needed.

Cobb Salad:
1. Preheat broiler or barbecue to 450 F. Place the prawns about 4 inches from the heat and grill until they are just firm and pink, 1½ to 2 minutes.
2. Remove from the heat and allow to cool. Shell prawns, leaving tails on.
3. Peel avocado and cut into ½-inch slices. In large bowl, gently toss green with the vinaigrette.

To Serve:
1. Arrange the salad greens on an oval-shaped serving plate. Keeping each ingredient separate, lay neat rows of blue cheese, tomatoes, avocado, spot prawns, egg and bacon on top of the greens. Serve immediately.

"You don't win friends with salad."
Homer Simpson

POTATO SOUP

Ingredients:
4 medium baking potatoes (about 2 lbs.)
¾ C. chopped onion
½ C. butter
½ C. all-purpose flour
½ tsp. dried basil
½ tsp. seasoned salt
¼ tsp. celery salt
¼ tsp. garlic powder
¼ tsp. onion salt
¼ tsp. pepper
¼ tsp. rubbed sage
¼ tsp. dried thyme
4½ C. chicken broth
6 C. milk
¾ to 1 C. grated Parmesan cheese
10 bacon strips, cooked and crumbled

Instructions:
1. Pierce potatoes with a fork; bake at 375° for 40-60 minutes until tender. Cool, peel and cube; set aside.

2. In a large Dutch oven or soup kettle, saute onion in butter until tender. Stir in flour and seasonings until blended. Gradually add broth, stirring constantly. Bring to a boil; cook and stir for 2 minutes or until thickened. Add potatoes; return to a boil. Reduce heat; cover and simmer for 10 minutes.

3. Add milk and cheese; heat through. Stir in bacon.

Signature Taste of VANCOUVER

6664 DEER LAKE AVENUE, BURNABY, BC

HART HOUSE

"My idea of heaven is a great big baked potato and someone to share it with."
Oprah Winfrey

VEGGIE BENEDICT

Signature Tastes of VANCOUVER

Inspired by the faded glory of Old Havana in Cuba, Havana opened its doors September 1996 in one of Vancouver's most diverse neighbourhoods. Havana is a unique part of Vancouver's cultural landscape, as it houses a Restaurant, Theatre and Gallery, all under the same roof. The Restaurant offers Nuevo Latino Cuisine and authentic Cuban cocktails in a funky, distressed, casual setting. Havana has a large well-heated all-weather award winning patio that is situated directly across from Grandview Park with a view of the city skyline and the Coastal Mountain Range.

Ingredients:
For the Hollandaise:
4 egg yolks
2 tsp. white wine
2 tsp. freshly squeezed lemon juice
2 lbs. clarified butter
2 C. hot water

For the Veggie Benedict:
1 English muffin
3 tbsp. unsalted butter
½ C. diced mushrooms
½ C. diced onions
1 tomato, thinly sliced
1 avocado, thinly sliced
Basted Eggs

Basted Eggs:
8-in. egg pan (recommended: Teflon-coated)
1 tsp. clarified butter
2 eggs
1 tbsp. water

Instructions:
1. In a stainless steel bowl, add the egg yolks, wine, and lemon juice. Place the stainless steel bowl over boiling water and whisk continuously until the yolks are thoroughly heated. It should be light and fluffy from all of the air that was whipped into it, but not scrambled. Remove from the heat.
2. Add a small amount of the hot water and whisk gently. *Cook's note: all whisking from this point on should be done gently to avoid breakage. Stream in the clarified butter slowly while whisking gently. Alternate between the butter and the hot water until the desired amount and consistency is achieved.
3. Butter the English muffin with 1 tablespoon of butter and toast it in a skillet until golden brown. In a separate medium skillet, saute the mushrooms and onions in the remaining butter. Place the tomato slices, avocado, mushrooms, and onions on top of the English muffin. Top it off with basted eggs and hollandaise sauce and serve.

Basted Eggs:
1. To make the basted eggs: Heat an 8-inch egg pan with 1 teaspoon of clarified butter. Add 2 eggs to the pan and cook until the whites are mostly cooked. Add 1 tablespoon of water and cover the eggs with a tight fitting lid to allow the eggs to cook with the steam. Cook until desired doneness.

HAVANA RESTAURANT & GALLERY

1212 COMMERCIAL DRIVE, VANCOUVER, BC

"I eat a variety of foods like vegetables, fruit and beef for protein and iron."
Sasha Cohen

CREPES SUZETTE HERMITAGE

Since its opening in 1988, The Hermitage has been a favourite of Vancouverites and visitors alike. Situated in an enclave away from the hustle and bustle of world famous Robson Street; it offers an elegant, but charmingly informal atmosphere that reflects the warmth and hospitality of provencal France.

Crepes:
2 tbsp. butter
1 C. flour
3 tbsp. sugar
⅛ tsp. salt
1¼ C. milk
1 egg, lightly beaten
1 tbsp. oil

Orange Sauce and Assembly:
juice of 6 oranges
½ C. apricot jam
¼ C. Grand Marnier
¼ C. (½ stick) butter
1 tsp. orange zest
vanilla ice cream, for serving
1 orange, peeled and separated into segments

Instructions:

Crepes:

1. Melt the butter over medium heat in a small skillet and cook until light brown. Strain through a fine mesh strainer and discard the solids.

2. Sift together the flour, sugar and salt into a large bowl.

3. Mix the milk and egg together and stir into the dry ingredients. Add the butter and stir to mix well. Set aside to rest 15 minutes.

4. Heat a medium non-stick skillet over medium heat. Brush lightly with oil. Pour ¼ cup of the batter into the skillet and tip back and forth to just coat the bottom. Cook until the edges just begin to turn brown and curl slightly, about 30 seconds.

5. Using a spatula to lift the edge, turn the crepe over and cook another 30 seconds.

6. Stack the finished crepes between sheets of parchment.

Orange Sauce and Assembly:

1. Bring the orange juice to a boil in a small saucepan. Add the apricot jam and cook to thicken, about 15 minutes. Add the Grand Marnier, butter and orange zest and simmer 5 more minutes.

2. To serve, place 1 small scoop of ice cream on each crepe. Fold the crepe in half, then fold in half again, to make a quarter. Put 2 crepes on each plate and warm in a 400-degree oven 1 minute.

3. Pour the sauce around the crepes and garnish each plate with 2 to 3 orange segments. Serve immediately before the ice cream melts.

1025 ROBSON STREET, #115, VANCOUVER, BC

HERMITAGE

"Food for the body is not enough. There must be food for the soul."
Dorothy Day

hidd n

MARTINI

CLASSIC	
vodka or gin, dash of white vermouth	
VANILLA COSMO	
vanilla vodka, cranberry juice, lime juice	
CRANTINI	
vodka, cranberry juice, and freshly squeezed lime juice	9
LITTLE MISS SUNSHINE	
vanilla vodka, malibu rum, amaretto, pineapple juice	9
LEMON DROP	
citron vodka, cointreau, fresh squeezed lime and lemon juice	9
BERRY SEXY	
blueberry vodka, crème de cassis, and fresh lime juice	9
PASSIONATE RAZZ	
raspberry vodka, alize, fresh lime juice, and a dash of soda	9
CELESTIAL EVENING	
vodka, banana liqueur, malibu, blue curacao, a splash of cranberry	9
PENNY LANE	
belvedere vodka, cointreau, pomegranate juice	
CHAMPAGNE	
ketel one vodka, champagne, and passion fruit alize	13
GREEN APPLE	
grey goose vodka, sourpuss, and lime juice	13
SUNSET	
grey goose l'orange, grand marnier, orange, cranberry & lime juice	13
FRENCH KISS	
grey goose, chambord, fresh pineapple juice	13
NEGRONI	
campari, bombay gin, sweet vermouth	13
TEN BERRY MARTINI	
tanqueray 10 with crème de cassis	13
BUDDHA'S HAND	
u'luvka, grand marnier, splash of lime and cranberry	17
AZTEC GOLD	
patron anejo, triple sec, cranberry juice, splash of lime juice	17
	17

Global
Leffe Blonde
Chimay Re
Chimay B
Mort S
Grolls
Hor
Cr

Caramelized Banana and Coconut Tart with Maker's Mark Ice Cream

Hidden Tasting Bar and Social Lounge offers something for everyone. A place to share food, and enjoy a unique beer or glass of wine in a relaxed environment. We have simplified the eating experience by integrating global food offerings using local ingredients, with attentive service. It's undeniably approachable, comfortable, and a place to rejuvenate.

Ingredients:

Tart Shell:
1¾ C. all-purpose flour
1 tbsp. sugar
½ tsp. salt
1 stick (½ C.) cold unsalted butter, cut into ½-inch cubes
¼ C. cold vegetable shortening
3 to 5 tablespoons ice water

Filling:
1½ C. of sugar
¼ C. of whipping cream
2 egg yolks
2 peeled bananas- chopped ½" thick pieces
¼ lb. unsalted butter
½ C. of coconut flakes

Ice cream:
1 C. of whipping cream
4 egg yolks
½ C. of sugar
1 oz. of Maker's Mark or high end whiskey

Instructions:

Tart Shell:
1. Blend together flour, sugar, salt, butter, and shortening with your fingertips or a pastry blender (or pulse in a food processor) just until most of mixture resembles coarse meal with small (roughly pea-size) butter lumps.
2. Drizzle evenly with 3 tablespoons ice water and gently stir with a fork (or pulse in food processor) until incorporated.
3. Squeeze a small handful: If it doesn't hold together, add more ice water, 1 tablespoon at a time, stirring (or pulsing) until just incorporated, then test again. (If you overwork mixture, pastry will be tough.)
4. Turn out mixture onto a lightly floured surface and divide into 6 portions. With heel of your hand, smear each portion once or twice in a forward motion. Gather dough together with scraper and press into a ball, then flatten into a 6-inch disk.
5. Chill, wrapped in plastic wrap, until firm, at least 1 hour.
6. Roll out dough with a floured rolling pin into a 13-inch round on a lightly floured surface and fit into tart pan.
7. Trim excess dough, leaving a ½-inch overhang, then fold overhang inward and press against side of pan to reinforce edge.
8. Lightly prick bottom and sides with a fork. Chill 30 minutes.
9. Preheat oven to 375°F. Line tart shell with foil or parchment paper and fill with pie weights. Bake in middle of oven until pastry is pale golden along rim, 20 minutes.
10. Carefully remove foil and weights and bake until pale golden all over, 10 minutes more. Cool in pan on a rack.

Filling:
1. In a small sauce pan, add 1 cup of the sugar. As the sugar melts it will begin to caramelize. When the sugar becomes a rich brown in colour add the whipping cream to make a caramel sauce. Set aside.
2. In a large sauce pan, melt the butter and add the chopped bananas. As the bananas cook they will begin to soften and brown. Add the remaining ½ cup of sugar and continue to cook the bananas until caramelized.
3. Remove from heat. Using a spoon, mash the bananas until all large chunks are softened (small pieces are ok).
4. Add the caramelized bananas evenly throughout the tart shell. Fill the tart shell with the caramel sauce. Sprinkle the top of the tart with the coconut flakes and bake in a 375°F oven for 18-20 minutes. Remove from oven and cool.

Ice Cream:
1. In a mixing bowl, whisk the sugar and egg yolks until well blended.
2. Scald the cream and slowly temper the cream into the egg-sugar mixture and add the whiskey.
3. Over a double boiler, place the cream mixture and stir using a rubber spatula. The cream mixture should thicken after approximately 10 minutes of stirring.
4. To test if the cream is thick enough, use your finger and draw a line through the back of the spatula. If the line holds then the cream is thickened. If not…keep stirring. Place the thickened cream mix in the freezer. Stir often until the liquids turns into ice cream.

"Life is like an ice-cream cone, you have to lick it one day at a time."
Charles M. Schulz

CHOCOLATE MOUSSE CAKE

Horizons is nestled in Burnaby Mountain Park amongst the lush green trees, beautiful rose gardens and majestic Japanese totem poles. The view from the Horizons dining room is only paralleled by the inventive West Coast cuisine created by Chef John Garrett.

Ingredients:
vegetable-oil cooking spray
²⁄₃ C. all-purpose flour
¹⁄₃ C. unsweetened Dutch-process cocoa powder
²⁄₃ C. sugar
½ tsp. baking soda
¾ tsp. baking powder
¼ tsp. salt
1 large egg, room temperature
¼ C. whole milk
3 tbsp. vegetable oil
½ tsp. pure vanilla extract
individual chocolate mousse
2 oz. solid semisweet chocolate

Instructions:
1. Preheat oven to 350 degrees. Place eight 6-ounce (3½-inch diameter) ramekins on a rimmed baking sheet, and coat with cooking spray; set aside.
2. Stir flour, cocoa powder, sugar, baking soda, baking powder, and salt in the bowl of an electric mixer. Attach bowl to mixer fitted with the paddle attachment. Add egg, milk, oil, vanilla, and ¼ cup water; mix on medium-low speed until smooth and combined, about 3 minutes.
3. Divide batter evenly among prepared ramekins. Bake until a cake tester inserted into the centers comes out clean, about 20 minutes. Transfer to a wire rack; let cool completely. Run a knife around sides of cakes; unmold. Cakes can be refrigerated, wrapped in plastic, up to 1 day.
4. Trim each cake to 1 inch high. Transfer to a baking sheet lined with parchment paper. Cut eight 10 ¾-by-4-inch strips of parchment paper. Wrap a parchment collar around base of each cake, keeping bottom flush with baking sheet. Secure each collar with tape; set aside.
5. Transfer bittersweet-chocolate mousse to a large pastry bag fitted with a large round tip (such as Ateco #808). Pipe a 1-inch layer of mousse into each parchment collar. Refrigerate until mousse is set, about 20 minutes. Repeat with milk chocolate mousse, piping on top of the bittersweet chocolate mousse. Refrigerate at least 4 hours and up to overnight.
6. Microwave semisweet chocolate until slightly warm but not melted, about 30 seconds. Scrape at a 45-degree angle with a vegetable peeler, forming curls. Before serving cakes, remove parchment collars, and garnish with chocolate curls.

HORIZONS
100 CENTENNIAL WAY, BURNABY, BC

"A great empire, like a great cake, is most easily diminished at the edges."
Benjamin Franklin

BAKED SALMON

Cosmopolitan. Urbane. Stylish. From the moment you arrive at the Four Diamond Hyatt Regency Vancouver, it will be clear that there's more here than meets the eye. Be treated to plush amenities and uncompromising service along with the largest guestrooms, most impressive meeting and event facilities, romantic wedding venues, and accomplished catering staff of any Vancouver, British Columbia hotel.

Ingredients:
2 lbs. salmon fillet
2 tbsp. horseradish
2 tbsp. dijon mustard
2 tbsp. oyster sauce
2 tbsp. chili sauce
1 tbsp. white wine
⅛ tsp. white pepper

Instructions:
1. Combine all ingredients. Pour over salmon, cover and refrigerate for at least 48 hours.

2. Bake skin side down in a buttered baking dish at 350 for 10 to 15 minutes.

HYATT REGENCY VANCOUVER
655 BURRARD STREET, VANCOUVER, BC

"You ain't supposed to get salmon when they're swimming upstream to spawn. But if you're hungry, you do."
Loretta Lynn

MINESTRONE SOUP

Although il Giardino sits in the heart of bustling downtown Vancouver, the natural, yet elegant decor, and home-like atmosphere makes the perfect place to relax, peruse our outstanding wine list and enjoy your dining experience. As in any good Italian home, your meal is always made from the freshest of ingredients. "If it is harvested today, it is eaten today." Come experience the flavours of Italy.

Ingredients:
1 - 1½ C. dried Cannellini or Great Northern Beans
2 oz. salt pork or pancetta
10 to 12 C. beef or chicken broth (use gluten-free broth for gluten-free version)
1 onion, chopped
1 celery stalk, chopped
1 carrot, chopped
2 garlic cloves, chopped
1 C. loosely packed parsley, chopped
½ C. extra virgin olive oil
½ head savoy or curly cabbage, sliced
1 potato, diced
2 zucchini, diced
2 carrots, diced
2 C. chopped Italian styled peeled plum tomatoes
salt and freshly ground black pepper
Parmesan cheese, grated for garnish

Instructions:

1. Soak beans overnight in cold water. Drain beans, rinse, and place them in a large saucepan or stockpot. Add salt pork or pancetta and 6 cups of broth. Cover and bring to a boil. Reduce heat and cook gently for about 1 hour.

2. Heat oil in a separate large stockpot. Add chopped vegetables (onion, celery, carrot, garlic, parsley) and sauté gently 5 to 8 minutes or until lightly browned. Add remaining vegetables and tomatoes. Add remaining 5 cups broth. Simmer for 40 to 50 minutes or until vegetables are tender.

3. Remove salt pork or pancetta from beans. Dice finely. Transfer half of the beans to a food processor or a blender and blend into a paste. Add mashed beans to the vegetables. Add remaining whole beans, broth, and diced pork to vegetables.

4. Simmer 5 minutes longer. Season soup with salt and pepper. Serve with a sprinkle of grated Parmesan cheese.

1382 HORNBY STREET, VANCOUVER, BC

IL GIARDINO

"Anyone who tells a lie has not a pure heart, and cannot make a good soup."
Ludwig van Beethoven

MARINATED SLICED RIBEYE

Signature Tastes of VANCOUVER

Ingredients:
1 (12 oz.) bottle red wine vinegar
1 tbsp. worcestershire sauce
1 tbsp. minced garlic
½ tbsp. minced onion
1 tsp. ground black pepper
2 (10 oz.) beef rib eye steaks

Instructions:

1. In a shallow, nonreactive dish, mix red wine vinegar, Worcestershire sauce, garlic, onion, and pepper. Place steaks in the mixture. Cover, and marinate 1 hour in the refrigerator.

2. Preheat an outdoor grill for high heat, and lightly oil grate.

3. Grill steaks on the prepared grill 5 to 7 minutes per side, to desired doneness. Discard remaining marinade.

INSADONG KOREAN BBQ
403 NORTH ROAD #301, COQUITLAM, BC

"The wise man should consider that health is the greatest of human blessings. Let food be your medicine."
Hippocrates

VEAL OSSU BUCCO

Signature Tastes of VANCOUVER

Ingredients:
1 12-14oz veal shank
½ C. mirepoix (carrot, celery, onion, garlic)
½ C. soaked and cooked cannellini beans
1 oz. ladle of toasted pinenuts
4 oz. yellow foot mushrooms
1 tbsp. roasted garlic
½ tbsp. sage leaves
1 tbsp. fine diced onion
1 oz. fine diced fennel
8 oz. ladle of veal jus
1 oz. ladle of Madeira
6 pcs. of grilled asparagus
season to taste

Instructions:

1. Season veal shank and sear in a hot pan with grape seed oil until golden brown.

2. Transfer veal shank into a pan that can go into the oven and add enough veal stock to cover veal shank as well as 1 cup of red wine, ½ cup of mirepoix, and 5 sprigs of thyme.

3. Cover pan with foil and cook in a pre heated oven at 325 degrees until finished. 2-4 hours.

4. Saute onion, garlic, fennel, mushrooms, and cannellini beans. Add Madeira, veal jus, sage, and pine nuts.

5. Finish with a teaspoon of butter and season. Season and oil asparagus. Grill asparagus.

6. Place ragu in bowl with asparagus on top and drape the veal shank on top with the jus.

ITALIAN KITCHEN
1037 ALBERNI STREET, VANCOUVER, BC

"Those who think they have no time for healthy eating will sooner or later have to find time for illness."
Edward Stanley

Joe Fortes Braised Beef Shortribs

In keeping with the reputation of the man whose name we adopted, Joe Fortes Seafood & Chop House has achieved legendary status in Vancouver. For 27 years, Joe Fortes has consistently earned and maintained its reputation as an award-winning Vancouver Restaurant and "Vancouver's Best Oyster Bar". This iconic Vancouver restaurant is conveniently located just off of bustling Robson Street. Joe Fortes is where locals and visitors alike come to enjoy the freshest seafood and chops in town, complemented by an award-winning wine list that boasts over 400 wines, and a uniquely personal level of service and hospitality.

Signature Tastes of VANCOUVER

Ingredients:
6 beef short ribs, 14 to 16 oz. each
1 tbsp. fresh thyme leaves
1 tbsp. freshly cracked black pepper
2 fresh bay leaves
1 C. diced onion
⅓ C. diced carrot
⅓ C. diced celery
sea salt
canola oil
3 C. red wine (one 750 ml bottle.....not Chateau Petrus)
6 C. beef or veal stock

Instructions:
1. Rinse and pat ribs dry with clean cloth.
2. Season short ribs with thyme, cracked black pepper and bay leaves, using your hands to coat the meat well.
3. Toss with diced vegetables and arrange, tightly packed, into large plastic container.
4. Cover with red wine and refrigerate overnight.
5. Preheat oven to 300 F.
6. Remove short ribs from wine mixture and drain well. Season generously on all sides with salt.
7. Heat a large sauté pan over high heat. Add 3 tablespoons oil and wait until the pan is very hot and almost smoking.
8. Working in batches, place short ribs in pan and sear until browned on all sides, about 6 minutes. Remove ribs to a braising pan.
9. Reduce heat to medium, add wine marinade and cook until reduced by half, scraping any bits left on sides of pan during searing.
10. Add stock to wine and bring to boil. Pour liquid over short ribs. Stock/wine mixture should almost cover ribs. Cover pot tightly with both foil and a lid and braise in the oven for 3½ to 4 hours.
11. Pierce a short rib with a paring knife to check for doneness; the meat should yield easily to the knife. Let ribs rest in their juices for 10 minutes, then transfer to a baking sheet.
12. Increase oven temperature to 400 F.
13. Place short ribs in the oven for 10 to 15 minutes to brown.
14. Strain broth into a saucepan, pressing down on the vegetables with a ladle to extract all the juices. Skim the fat from the sauce. If the broth seems thin, reduce it over medium-high heat to thicken slightly. Taste for seasoning.
15. Serve with your favourite potatoes or fresh bread.

777 Thurlow Street, Vancouver, BC

Joe Fortes

"Gluttony is an emotional escape, a sign something is eating us."
Peter De Vries

SAUTEED CRIMINI MUSHROOMS

The Keg Steakhouse & Bar serves the finest cuts of succulent steak, aged for tenderness and grilled to perfection. Prime rib is a Keg specialty; slow roasted, hand carved and perfectly seasoned with special Keg spices. The restaurant also serves delicious seafood, memorable appetizers, crisp salads... and decadent desserts.

Ingredients:
1 tbsp. extra-virgin olive oil, 1 turn of the pan
2 tbsp. butter
1½ lbs. crimini mushrooms, brushed clean with damp towel
salt and pepper
3 tbsp. fresh thyme leaves, chopped
½ C. dry red wine
2 tbsp. chopped fresh parsley leaves

Instructions:

1. Heat a large skillet over medium high heat.

2. Add extra-virgin olive oil and butter.

3. Add mushrooms and season with salt, pepper and thyme then cook 15 minutes until evenly browned and tender.

4. Add wine and deglaze the pan.

5. Add parsley and transfer mushrooms to a serving dish.

KEG STEAKHOUSE & BAR
742 THURLOW STREET, VANCOUVER, BC

"You must grow like a tree, not like a mushroom."
Janet Erskine Stuart

BEEFSTEAK & HEIRLOOM TOMATO SALAD

Signature Taste of VANCOUVER

Kitsilano Daily Kitchen: A fresh approach to unpretentious West Coast Cuisine. Daily visits to the local markets and farms of British Columbia to procure the finest local seafood, produce and meats at the peak of quality. Working the best the West Coast has to offer and prepping, cooking and creating a new menu every day. Always in the season, local and organic whenever possible.

Ingredients:
3 ripe beefsteak
tomatoes, cut into
½-inch thick slices
12 seedless watermelon
sticks (3 in. long sticks)
8 sticks firm feta cheese
(2 in. long sticks)
4 tbsp. extra virgin olive
oil (good quality)
4 tbsp. balsamic vinegar
basil leaves
sea salt or herb fleur de
sel
2 C. fresh basil leaves
1 C. olive oil
salt, to taste

Instructions:

1. To prepare Basil Oil: blanch 2 cups basil leaves in boiling water, then immediately place in ice water; drain well.

2. Transfer drained basil to blender; add 1 cup olive oil and salt to taste; process 1 minute or until pureed.

3. Pass through a fine mesh strainer.

4. To prepare the salad, divide tomato slices among four salad plates.

5. Top each with three sticks watermelon and two sticks feta cheese; drizzle with olive oil, balsamic vinegar and some basil oil.

6. Garnish with basil leaves; serve salt separately.

KITSILANO DAILY KITCHEN
1809 W 1ST AVE. VANCOUVER, BC

"The only time to eat diet food is while you're waiting for the steak to cook."
Julia Child

Warm Steelhead and Crunchy Potato Salad

L''Abattoir is located in the center of Gastown between historic Gaoler's Mews and Blood Alley. The restaurant was built in the 19th century and is the site of Vancouver's first jail. Originally buttressed to the city's main butchery and meat packing district, the name L'Abattoir pays homage to the neighbourhood's colourful past.

Signature Tastes of VANCOUVER

217 CARRALL STREET, VANCOUVER, BC

L'ABATTOIR

Ingredients
12 oz. steelhead fillet (sub trout or salmon if steelhead not available)
1 large starchy potato (yukon gold/russet/kennebec)
4 oz. mayonnaise
2 oz. Dijon mustard
1 head pickled garlic slices
4 pcs. assorted radishes
2 soft boiled eggs
½ C. loosely packed fresh dill leaves
½ C. baby cabbage greens
1 lemon for juicing
1 pc. fresh horseradish root
extra virgin olive oil
oil for deep frying
salt and pepper

Instructions:

1. Simmer potato in salted water until completely cooked through. Allow to cool, break apart into bite-size pieces, and reserve.

2. Place boneless/skinless steelhead fillet on an oiled baking sheet and season with salt and pepper. Place in 250°F oven for 12 minutes or until the fish becomes opaque in colour and just slightly firm to the touch. Remove fish from oven and set aside to rest.

3. Heat frying oil to 350°F and fry cooked potato pieces until golden and crunchy. Drain on to paper towel and season with salt.

4. Mix mayonnaise and dijon mustard together and set aside.

5. Thinly slice radishes and season with salt and olive oil.

To Assemble:

1. Spoon mustard and mayonnaise mixture onto the plates and place fried potatoes on top.

2. Break steelhead into bite size pieces and distribute evenly amongst the fried potatoes.

3. Cut soft boiled eggs in half and season with salt and pepper; place one half on each dish.

4. Arrange pickled garlic slices and radish slices neatly on each dish.

5. Dress cabbage greens and dill leaves lightly in olive oil and lemon juice; arrange on each dish.

6. Grate fresh horseradish over the salad, as much or as little as you like.

"I think someone should have had the decency to tell me the luncheon was free. To make someone run out with potato salad in his hand, pretending he's throwing up, is not what I call hospitality."
Jack Handy

POACHED PHEASANT WITH BERRIES

La Belle Auberge Restaurant is located in the old village of Ladner, British Columbia. It is situated in a 100-year-old Victorian house. The restaurant has two levels and five dining rooms. All dining rooms can be enclosed for private functions and seat up to 100 guests. La Belle Auberge is one of four Mobil Exxon 4-stars in Vancouver and it has also won many awards. La Belle Auberge Restaurant is providing cooking classes through a 4-course gastronomic menu format to the public. Classes will be held Sundays or Mondays. Check our COOKING CLASSES link for more information.

Ingredients:
1½ C. dry white wine
2 tbsp. juniper berries
1 tsp. black peppercorns
1 (2½- to 3-lb.) domestic pheasant
salt and freshly ground pepper to taste
6 tbsp. butter
2 carrots, finely chopped
1 medium onion, finely chopped
2 garlic cloves, finely chopped
¼ lb. pancetta, cut into 4 slices and diced
gated zest of 1 lemon
1 tbsp. all-purpose flour
⅓ C. gin
juice of 1 lemon

Instructions:
1. Combine wine, juniper berries and peppercorns in a small bowl. Let stand 2 hours.
2. Wash and dry pheasant thoroughly. Season with salt and pepper inside bird and outside. Tie firmly with kitchen twine to retain its shape.
3. Melt 5 tablespoons butter in a large heavy casserole. When butter foams, add pheasant breast-side down. Brown on all sides over medium heat.
4. Add carrots, onion, garlic and pancetta. Saute until lightly browned.
5. Drain juniper berries and peppercorns, reserving wine. Crush juniper berries and peppercorns.
6. Pour wine over pheasant. When wine is reduced by half, add juniper berries, peppercorns and lemon zest. Cover casserole.
7. Cook over medium heat 1½ hours or until pheasant is tender. Place pheasant on a cutting board.
8. Combine 1 tablespoon butter and flour and work into a small ball. Raise heat.
9. Stir gin and lemon juice into casserole.
10. Add butter-flour ball and mix until well blended, about 1 minute.
11. Press sauce through a sieve into a warm bowl.
12. Cut pheasant into 4 pieces. Arrange on a warm platter.
13. Taste and adjust sauce for seasoning, then spoon over pheasant.

"One cannot think well, love well, sleep well, if one has not dined well."
Virginia Woolf

Cured Duck with Gorgonzola Cheese + Figs

La Brasserie is a 35-seat Franco-German restaurant situated in the heart of Vancouver's West End. Brothers Michael and Stephen Wiese have given Davie St. a cozy neighborhood gem that showcases the best of French and German comfort food.

Ingredients:
24 slices cured duck breast
8 figs
100g gorgonzola cheese
25mL sherry vinegar
75mL extra virgin olive oil
1 shallot
1 bunch arugula
salt + pepper to taste

Instructions:
1. Mince shallot very fine.

2. Combine shallot + vinegar.

3. Slowly whisk in olive oil.

4. Slice figs into quarters.

5. Arrange figs, sliced duck breast + gorgonzola cheese on plate.

6. Dress arugula in a bowl.

7. Drizzle dressing over salad.

8. Garnish with arugula.

La Brasserie
1091 Davie Street, Vancouver, BC

"You have to be a romantic to invest yourself, your money, and your time in cheese."
Anthony Bourdain

Nestled on the edge of Vancouver's historic Yaletown, La Terrazza Restaurant has been impressing diners since 1998. Located close to most major venues including GM Place, BC Place, and the Queen Elizabeth Theatre. La Terrazza boasts some of Vancouver's most sought after cuisine and an internationally renowned wine list.

Ingredients:
½ lb. white chocolate melted
1½ lbs. cream cheese
1¼ C. sugar granulated
1½ tsp. orange zest grated
3 large eggs
½ C. cream
3 tbsp. cream
½ tsp. vanilla extract
12 each phyllo pastry sheets
1 x butter melted
sour cherry for toppings

Instructions:
1. While chocolate melts in double boiler, use a mixer on low smooth. (Do not use low-fat cheese in this recipe)
2. Beat in eggs one at a time, followed by cream and vanilla.
3. Add a little of the cheese mixture to the warmed chocolate, then stir this mixture into remaining cheese mixture.
4. Spoon mixture into a buttered 9-inch layer cake pan, lined with parchment paper.
5. Set in a pan, and pour in hot water until it reaches halfway up the pan.
6. Bake in a 350 F. oven, adding more water if needed, until set and lightly browned on top, about 1 hour.
7. Remove from oven, let cool, and refrigerate for at least 4 hours.
8. To serve, lightly brush each 8 - 12 inch square of phyllo pastry with melted butter.
9. Gently remove each slice of cheesecake from pan.
10. Wrap a sheet of prepared phyllo pastry around each piece, folding until cake is covered with three layers.
11. Trim excess pastry.
12. Brush each dessert with additional melted butter.
13. Place on a baking sheet and bake in a 350 F oven for 10 minutes, or until phyllo begins to brown.
14. Transfer to dessert plates and decorate with sour cherry.

1088 CAMBIE STREET, VANCOUVER, BC

LA TERRAZZA

"If food were free, why work?"
Douglas Horton

At Las Margaritas you'll find what's been called the city's best salsa and margaritas, as well as the largest tequila selection in B.C. Las Margaritas serves up hearty portions and the price range is hard to beat. Owner Dan Rodriguez and general manager Rolando Guardia serve food more from the north of Mexico, Baja and California. Rodriguez frequently visits Mexico, Southern California and the Baja to make sure his restaurant keeps up with current trends in Mexican food and drinks.

Ingredients:
2 lbs. of firm, fresh red snapper fillets (or other firm-fleshed fish), cut into ½ in pieces, completely deboned
½ C. of fresh squeezed lime juice
½ C. of fresh squeezed lemon juice
½ red onion, finely diced
1 C. of chopped fresh seeded tomatoes
1 serrano chili, seeded and finely diced
2 tsp. of salt
dash of ground oregano
dash of Tabasco or a light pinch of cayenne pepper
cilantro
avocado
tortillas or tortilla chips

Instructions:

1. In a non-reactive casserole dish, either Pyrex or ceramic, place the fish, onion, tomatoes, chili, salt, Tabasco, and oregano. Cover with lime and lemon juice. Let sit covered in the refrigerator for an hour, then stir, making sure more of the fish gets exposed to the acidic lime and lemon juices. Let sit for several hours, giving time for the flavors to blend.

2. During the marinating process the fish will change from pinkish grey and translucent, to whiter in color and opaque.

3. Serve with chopped cilantro and slices of avocado with heated tortillas for ceviche tacos or with tortilla chips.

LAS MARGARITAS MEXICAN

1999 WEST 4TH AVENUE, VANCOUVER, BC

"If you really want to make a friend, go to someone's house and eat with him... the people who give you their food give you their heart."
Cesar Chavez

LE CROCODILE ONION TART

Impeccable service with flair, never pretense or fanfare. Le Crocodile blends traditional French cooking with innovative Westcoast style. Michel has cooked for and seen generation after generation of families pass through the doors of Le Crocodile. Twenty-five years later, with some of the original staff still here, Le Crocodile still remains in Vancouver as one of the city's most acclaimed and visited restaurants.

Ingredients:
1 10-in. pie shell
5 onions, peeled and sliced in long, extra fine strips
4 tbsp. butter
1 tbsp. vegetable oil
2 tbsp. flour
2 C. milk
4 eggs, well beaten
8 oz. bacon, chopped fine and fried
1 C. whipping cream
1 pinch salt
several grindings of freshly ground pepper
dash of nutmeg

Instructions:
1. In a large skillet with high sides cook the onions in the oil and 2 tbsp. of the butter until onions are transparent. Do not brown.
2. Remove from heat and set aside.
3. Melt the remaining 2 tbsp. of butter in a saucepan. Add the flour and cook slowly, stirring, until the butter and flour froth together for one minute without coloring. Whisking all the time, add the milk and stir until the sauce comes to a boil. Pour this mixture over the top of the onions and return the onions to the heat.
4. Add the eggs, bacon and whipped cream, stirring well after each addition. Season with salt, pepper and nutmeg. Pour this mixture into the prepared pie shell and cook on the bottom shelf of the oven for approximately one hour at 400 F.
5. Test tart to see if it is thoroughly cooked by giving it a gentle shake. If it is still wobbly in the center, turn off the heat and leave in the closed oven for another 30 minutes. The golden surface color can be protected from further browning by placing a sheet of aluminum foil over the top of the pie. Serve warm but it is delicious cold!

909 BURRARD STREET, VANCOUVER, BC

LE CROCODILE

"All we have to do is to peel the shrines like an onion, and we will be with the king himself."
Howard Carter

Les Faux Bourgeois

TRO

CAFE

shermansfood

Escargots de Bourgogne

"Uncork the wine, enjoy the dance, and let the Gods decide the rest!" Horace's words are even more emphatic as we muddle through another wet Spring! Soon we will bid adieu to the lamb stews and Cassoulets, and welcome the fresh Halibut, the Spot Prawns, the 'uni', the wild mushrooms, and all the wonderful Northwest ingredients which find their way to our kitchen. Thanks to the readers of the Westender for choosing Les Fauxbo as their favourite French destination in the city, and for wonderful kudos from both The Courier and The Georgia Straight (Stars of 2012 and Golden Plates 2012).

Ingredients:
1½ bunches parsley, stems removed
4 garlic cloves, roughly chopped
1 tsp. salt, or to taste
1 lb. butter, diced into small cubes, cold

Instructions:
1. Place the parsley, garlic, and salt in a food processor fitted with a metal chopping blade and pulse until evenly minced and well blended.

2. Add the cubed butter to the parsley-garlic mixture. Process, scraping down the sides as needed, until the butter is softened and mixture is well blended. The butter should be light green in color.

3. The butter may be placed into a ramekin, or shaped into a log and rolled in plastic wrap. Refrigerate until ready for use. The butter can be held for at least a week in the refrigerator, or frozen for several weeks.

LES FAUX BOURGEOIS
663 E 15TH AVE, VANCOUVER, BC

"Know how to garnish food so that it is more appealing to the eye and even more flavorful than before."
Marilyn vos Savant

STUFFED PORK CHOPS

After hosting Licence to Grill seen on Food Network Canada, Discovery Home in the U.S., Asian Food Channel across Asia and now in syndication, Rainford has spent the last two years quietly perfecting his signature style "The Rainford Method". Experience this Method in his newest cookbook - Born to Grill.

Ingredients:
10 to 12 oz large pork chops (bone in)
3 tbsp. olive oil
4 clove garlic (minced)
½ tsp. sage (finely chopped)
2 Granny Smith apples (small dice)
3 slices bacon (cut into small pieces)
1 shallot (small dice)
½ rib celery (small dice)
½ C. shitake mushrooms (thin slices)
½ C. oyster mushrooms (thin slices)
1 C. spinach (quickly sautéed)
TT kosher salt
TT black pepper (freshly cracked)

Instructions:
This recipe requires you to do a little work ahead of time but boy will you enjoy your effort when you're eating perfectly grilled chops.
1. To prepare the pork take a boning knife and make a little pocket in the meat side. Run your knife so as to not to butterfly the meat but to create a pocket so you can stuff the content inside without it coming out while it's grilling.
2. Place a cast iron pan on the grill and pre heat. The bacon will be the first thing going into the pan. Just slice the bacon into small pieces and cook until done but still soft.
3. Next add the shallots and celery and sweat until soft (no color).
4. Follow the previous steps by adding the mushrooms followed by the spinach this will only take about 15 to 20 second to wilt. Cool the mixture and then stuff each chop individually.
5. Place the pork at the 12 o'clock position and then turn to the 3 o'clock position. This will give the pork the perfect grill marks. Flip the pork over and place on the medium low side approx 300 degrees F to finish cooking.

LICENSE TO GRILL
ROB RAINFORD'S RECIPE

"There is poetry in a pork chop to a hungry man."
Philip Gibbs

Signature Tastes of VANCOUVER

Patti Lombardo opened Lombardo's in 1986. For 25 years she has served up some of the best pizza in the city. Many awards and accolades have been attributed to the Napoletana style of wood-oven pizza. Long standing aficionados come to enjoy the thin crisp pizza cooked to perfection. The use of fresh, local ingredients lend themselves to a high quality pizza.

Ingredients:
8 C. of chicken broth (keep one cold in the fridge)
3 eggs
3 tbsp. parmesan cheese
3 tbsp. of semolina flour

Instructions:
1. Start to boil seven cups of the broth but keep one cold in the fridge.
2. While the broth is starting to boil take the three eggs, the cheese and the semolina flour and mix (not whisk) it together in a bowl.
3. Once the mixture is well blended add one cup of the cold broth.
4. Now beat together as if you were scrambling eggs.
5. Once the water starts to boil, let it keep boiling and then stir it with a whisk to form a whirlpool.
6. Keep the whirlpool going with the whisk as you slowly pour the egg mixture in the boiling broth.
7. Use the whisk to "scramble" the broth. After a few minutes stop whisking and you will see little shreds in the broth (hence the name "stracciatella" which comes from the Italian verb "stracciare" which means "to shred"
8. Serve with additional parmesan cheese if desired.

LOMBARDO'S RISTORANTE
1641 COMMERCIAL DRIVE, VANCOUVER, BC

"Maybe a person's time would be as well spent raising food as raising money to buy food."
Frank Howard Clark

STRACCIATELLA

Patti lombardo opened Lombardo's in 1986. For 25 years she has served up some of the best pizza in the city. Many awards and accolades have been attributed to the Napolateana style of wood-oven pizza. Long standing affecienados come to enjoy the thin crisp pizza cooked to perfection. The use of fresh, local ingredients lend themselves to a high quality pizza.

Ingredients:
8 C. of chicken broth
(keep one cold in the fridge)
3 eggs
3 tbsp. parmesan cheese
3 tbsp. of semolina flour

Instructions:
1. Start to boil seven cups of the broth but keep one cold in the fridge.
2. While the broth is starting to boil take the three eggs, the cheese and the semolina flour and mix (not whisk) it together in a bowl.
3. Once the mixture is well blended add one cup of the cold broth.
4. Now beat together as if you were scrambling eggs.
5. Once the water starts to boil, let it keep boiling and then stir it with a whisk to form a whirlpool.
6. Keep the whirlpool going with the whisk as you slowly pour the egg mixture in the boiling broth.
7. Use the whisk to "scramble" the broth. After a few minutes stop whisking and you will see little shreds in the broth (hence the name "stracciatella" which comes from the Italian verb "stracciare" which means "to shred"
8. Serve with additional parmesan cheese if desired.

1641 COMMERCIAL DRIVE, VANCOUVER, BC

LUPO

"Maybe a person's time would be as well spent raising food as raising money to buy food."
Frank Howard Clark

Plah Tort Samun Plai

Simplicity, innovation and balance are the key ingredients in chef Angus An's philosophy behind the authentic Thai dishes served at Maenam. His menu is rooted in balancing intense fresh flavours with seasonal ingredients and locally sourced products, while respecting the tradition and the origin of each recipe. With inspiration found in continuous travel, the menu at Maenam is ever-changing but always served with Thai flare and enjoyed in its traditional context, be it family style dining or riffs on Thai street food.

Ingredients:
150 g lingcod
Corn starch
2-3 tbsp. caramelized tamarind sauce
1 tsp. fried lemongrass
1 tsp. fried green peppercorn
1 tsp. fried dried bird's eye chillies
1 tsp. fried galangal
1 tsp. fried shallots
1 tsp. fried garlic
4 halfs of fried kaffir lime leaf

Instructions:

1. Score the fish on the flesh side so once fried it will bend slightly.

2. Coat with corn starch well, and fry until crispy and cooked.

3. In a pan, or wok, heat up some sauce, toss with the fish and toss in all the spices until evenly coated.

1938 West 4th Avenue, Vancouver, BC

Maenam

"My weaknesses have always been food and men - in that order."
Dolly Parton

KAKI FRY

Maguro is the original Japanese sushi restaurant conveniently located in Ladner, Delta near Tsawwassen & Delta BC Ferries Terminal. Enjoy the convenience of a constant parade of diverse sushi dishes, maki rolls, cones, and sashimi dishes, traditional Japanese preparations or our own special creations. Enjoy the show as our two master sushi chiefs dexterously prepare sushi.

Signature Tastes of VANCOUVER

Ingredients:
16 oysters
2 eggs
1 C. panko (bread crumb)
¼ C. flour
oil for frying
salt and pepper to season
julienned cabbage

Instructions:

1. Clean oysters in salted water. Dry oysters with paper towels. Sprinkle salt and pepper over oysters. Put flour, beaten eggs, and panko in separate plates. Coat oysters with flour, eggs, then panko. Fry oysters in 350 degrees F oil until turn brown. Place julienned cabbage on a plate and serve fried oysters on the side.

2. Once the paneer is cool enough to handle with your hands, gently squeeze out the sugar syrup from the paneer and place the paneer into a serving dish.

3. Pour the prepared reduced milk over the paneer and chill in the refrigerator.

4. Garnish with additional chopped nuts.

5241 LADNER TRUNK ROAD, DELTA, BC

MAGURO SUSHI

"Never order food in excess of your body weight."
Erma Bombeck

ZUPPA AROMA

Signature Tastes of VANCOUVER

Mangia E Bevi Ristorante offers a classic Italian menu, a warm and inviting ambience, patio seating (weather permitting) and the passion of owners Antonio Sauro, Robert Parrott and Doug Grisdale to provide a memorable fine dining experience.

Ingredients:
Leek and Forest Mushroom Soup:
¼C. butter
1 tbsp. olive oil
1 white onion, finely diced
2 cloves garlic, finely diced
2 leeks, whites only, finely chopped
2 sprigs fresh thyme
2 sprigs fresh tarragon
1 C. white wine
¼ C. sherry
2 C. mixed forest mushrooms (buttons, Crimini, Oysters and Chanterelle mushrooms)
2 C. chicken or vegetable stock
1 C. whipping cream
2 tbsp. dark soya sauce
1 tbsp. sherry wine vinegar
¼ C. parmesan cheese, grated
coarse salt and freshly ground black pepper to taste

Olive Oil and Parmesan Crostini:
½ baguette, sliced on an angle ½-inch thick
olive oil, as needed
½ C. parmesan cheese, grated
coarse salt

Instructions:
Leek and Forest Mushroom Soup:
1. Combine the butter, olive oil, onion, garlic and leeks in a large soup pot. Sweat for about 2 minutes.
2. Add thyme, tarragon, white wine and sherry, cover and place over medium-high heat. Allow the mixture to cook until the onions are soft and translucent (about 7 – 8 minutes).
3. Remove the lid and add the mushrooms. Cook the mushrooms, until they begin to sweat and lose volume (about 2 – 3 minutes).
4. Add the stock and whipping cream and bring the mixture to a simmer.
5. Add the soya sauce and allow the mixture to cook for an additional 10 – 15 minutes.
6. Add the sherry wine vinegar and season the soup with coarse salt and freshly ground pepper.
7. Blend the mixture in a standing blender until it is uniform and smooth. Serve hot with sprinkled Parmesan cheese.

Olive Oil and Parmesan Crostini:
1. On a baking tray, lightly drizzle olive oil on both sides of the baguette slices, and then season with coarse salt.
2. Evenly sprinkle the grated parmesan over the top of the baguette slices.
3. Bake the bread in a 400 degree oven until golden brown. Serve alongside the soup.

2222 MARINE DRIVE, WEST VANCOUVER, BC

MANGIA E BEVI

"Once, during Prohibition, I was forced to live for days on nothing but food and water."
W. C. Fields

BUTTERNUT SQUASH SOUP

MARKET by Jean-Georges is the hotel's signature restaurant, offering four distinct dining atmospheres with particular emphasis on fresh local seafood. Xi Shi Lounge features dramatic two-storey floor-to-ceiling windows overlooking an outdoor art galleria, curated by the Vancouver Art Gallery. At the lounge, diners can also linger over live piano music and sip premium liquor or opt for a lavish afternoon tea. Get healthy drinks from Ginger Juice Bar to sip outdoors or by the pool.

Ingredients:
For Mushroom Mousse:
¼ C. dried porcini mushrooms
½ C. boiling water
½ C. heavy cream

For Butternut Squash Soup:
4 C. gf chicken stock
1 butternut squash (about 2 lbs.), peeled, seeded & cut into 1 in. dice
1 C. heavy cream
2 parsley sprigs
2 small sage sprigs
1 bay leaf
dash freshly grated nutmeg
dash cayenne pepper
salt & freshly ground black pepper

Garnish:
2 tbsp. fresh chives, chopped
dash cayenne

Instructions:
1. In a small bowl, soak porcini mushrooms in boiling water until softened, about 20-30 minutes.
2. Meanwhile, in a large saucepan, combine stock with butternut squash, parsley, sage and bay leaf. Bring to a boil. Reduce heat and simmer for 20 minutes or until squash is very tender. Discard parsley, sage and bay leaf.
3. Working in batches, using a blender, puree squash and stock.
4. Return puree to saucepan and add 1 cup heavy cream. Stir to combine. Add nutmeg and cayenne. Adjust seasonings to taste with salt and freshly ground black pepper. Keep warm over low heat.
5. Transfer soaked mushrooms to a blender along with soaking liquid (discarding any sediment) and puree. Season to taste with salt and freshly ground black pepper.
6. In a medium bowl, whip cream until firm. Fold in mushroom puree and adjust seasonings to taste with salt and freshly ground black pepper.
7. To serve, ladle soup into shallow soup bowls. Dollop mushroom mousse in center. Garnish with chopped chives and a dash of cayenne.

MARKET BY JEAN-GEORGES
1128 W GEORGIA ST, VANCOUVER, BC

Signature Taste of VANCOUVER

"I live on good soup, not on fine words."
Moliere

BUTTER CHICKEN

Maurya Indian Cuisine is the new landmark of fine dining in Vancouver. Serving exotic, mouth watering dishes, Maurya balances flavour with healthy cuisine using minimal oils, butter and creams. Using a base of five "mother sauces" instead of the usual one, Maurya's splendid cuisine is light while still keeping the flame of traditional Indian cuisine burning bright. Each dish is prepared & served in the same manner as it was made really for the Maharajas and Nawabs (Emperors) of India.

Ingredients:
2 C. butter chicken sauce pre made at the restaurant
1 tbsp. kasoori methi (fenugreek powder)
4 tbsp. cream
1 tsp. of salt
1 tsp. of sugar
10 cubes of Pre cooked chicken cooked in our traditional clay oven.*

*People can make this chicken at home in an oven.

Instructions:
1. We will pour the sauce in a pan and then once it gets warm, add chicken. Once the chicken is fully hot add a dash of cream and then sprinkle the fenugreek powder add sugar and salt.

2. Stir and serve.

MAURYA INDIAN CUISINE
1643 WEST BROADWAY, VANCOUVER, BC

Signature Tastes of VANCOUVER

"Regard it as just as desirable to build a chicken house as to build a cathedral."
Frank Lloyd Wright

ASSORTED TEMPURA

Fresh ingredients, global inspiration and artful presentation are the benchmarks of Miku Restaurant's outstanding, innovative cuisine. From its signature Aburi-style sushi, lightly seared and infused with savoury sauces to its tantalizing meats, tenderized by Sumiyaki grilling, and desserts created by its Kyoto-trained pastry chef, Miku introduces cutting-edge culinary techniques to Vancouver.

Ingredients:
1 small sweet potato (about 115 g. or 4 oz.)
8 large tiger prawns (shrimp)
1 small squid, cleaned
vegetable oil, for deep frying
flour, for coating
1 small carrot, cut into matchsticks
4 shiitake mushrooms, stems removed
50 g./2 oz french beans
1 red bell pepper, seeded and sliced into ¾ inch thick strips

For the Dip:
200 ml/7 fluid ounces/ 1 C. water
45 ml/3 tbsp. mirin (sweet rice wine)
10 g./¼ oz. bonito flakes
45 ml/3 tbsps. japanese soy sauce

For the Batter:
1 egg
90 ml/6 tbsp. iced water
75 g./3 oz. /¾ C. plain (all-purpose) flour
2.5 ml/½ tsp. baking powder

Instructions:
1. Mix the dip ingredients in a pan. Bring to the boil, cool, then strain. Divide among 4-6 bowls.
2. Slice the unpeeled sweet potato thinly. Put in a bowl with cold water to cover.
3. Peel the prawns, leaving the tail shells intact, and de-vein. Lay a prawn on its side. Make three or four diagonal slits, about two-thirds of the way in towards the spine, leaving all the pieces attached. Repeat with the rest. Flatten with your fingers.
4. Cut the body of the squid into 3 cm/1¼ inch thick strips.
5. Put the egg in a large bowl, stir without beating and set half aside. Add the iced water, flour and baking powder. Stir two or three times, leaving some flour unblended.
6. Heat the oil in a deep fryer to 185 degrees C/ 365 degrees F. Dust the prawns lightly with flour. Holding each in turn by the tail, dip them into the batter, then carefully lower them into the hot oil; cook until golden.
7. Fry the remaining prawns and the squid in the same way. Keep warm.
8. Reduce the temperature of tile oil to 170 degrees C/ 340 degrees F. Drain the sweet potato and pat dry. Dip the vegetables into the batter and deep fry. Drain well, then keep warm and serve with the dip.

1055 WEST HASTINGS STREET, VANCOUVER, BC

MIKU RESTAURANT

"Our minds are like our stomachs; they are whetted by the change of their food, and variety supplies both with fresh appetite."
Quintilian

Curry Cornmeal Crusted Scallops with Corn Succotash

Signature Tastes of Vancouver

Mistral showcases uncomplicated French cuisine, highlighted with the season's finest ingredients. Inspired by the wind that sweeps through the south of France, our decor is reminiscent of Provence, with hand picked pottery and arched windows that evoke warmth and sophistication.

Ingredients:
Corn Puree
8 cups corn, off the cob

Corn Succotash:
1 tbsp. olive oil
2 bell peppers, diced
2 tsp. Dale Mackay's Mexican Spice Blend (or your own)
3 sprigs chervil, finely chopped
2 C. corn kernels

Corn Puree:
1 tbsp. cream
scallops w/ curry cornmeal crust
12 scallops
1 C. coarse cornmeal
¼ C. Dale Mackay's Canadian Curry powder

Sauce*:
¼ C. scallop trim
8 shallots, rough chop
3 liters Double chicken jus (or brown chicken stock)
white wine vinegar
aromatics

Garnish:
roasted mushrooms
sea asparagus

Scallop trim might be tough to come by, so rest assured, this dish sings well enough without the sauce. If you can wrangle the trim from a fishmonger though, do so.

Instructions:
Corn Puree:
1. Blend the corn kernels for approximately 3 minutes on high-speed in blender until pulped. Strain through a fine chinois or cheese cloth, pressing the juice from the remaining pulp. In a rounded bottom pan, cook the strained juices over low–medium heat whisking constantly as the starches will catch on the bottom. Cook until natural starches have thickened and the flavours of the starches have dissipated, approximately 15 minutes. Strain, cover and cool.

Succotash:
1. In a hot pan add a splash of oil and quickly sauté the bell peppers. Once the rawness of the peppers is gone, add the Mexican Spice Blend and cook for a few seconds more to toast the spices. To assemble, combine in a pot: the corn, a splash of cream and the bell peppers. Heat with a splash of water until the corn is just under cooked. Add corn puree and splash of water to the desired consistency and finish with chopped chervil.

Scallop Jus:
1. In a pan over very high heat, roast scallop trim to caramelize. Once a deep color has developed, add shallots and sweat. Add aromatics (coriander, peppercorns and thyme).
2. Deglaze with vinegar and reduce until a glaze. Add double chicken stock and bring to a simmer. Skim regularly and pass through a fine chinois when desired consistency has been reached. Ideally, the sauce should hold the plate without pooling.

Scallops with Curry Cornmeal Crust:
1. Combine in a bowl the cornmeal and curry powder before pressing scallops firmly into the crust mix. Sear the scallops over medium-high heat for 1.5 minutes per side until coloured and cooked.

Assembly:
1. Put down a bed of the succotash; place the scallops on top. Garnish with the roasted mushrooms and sea asparagus; and drizzle the scallop jus around.

2585 West Broadway, Vancouver, BC

Mistral Bistro

"Playwrights are like men who have been dining for a month in an Indian restaurant. After eating curry night after night, they deny the existence of asparagus."
Peter Ustinov

Signature Tastes of VANCOUVER

The Naam is a very busy vegetarian full-service restaurant located in the heart of Vancouver's Kitsilano district. It is the city's oldest natural foods restaurant, with over 30 years of cooking tradition. The Naam is "funky" wooden tables, an old wooden floor, and casual decor. In the winter we burn through about six cords of wood in our fireplace. In the summer we have a beautiful enclosed (or open as weather permits) garden patio, an extremely popular place on warm balmy evenings. We have live music every night from 7-10 pm - mostly blues, folk and jazz.

Ingredients:
4 medium sized croissants
2 plum tomatoes, thinly sliced
4 eggs
1 tbsp. milk
salt
freshly ground pepper
1½ tsp. butter
4 slices Havarti cheese, cut in half diagonally

Instructions:
1. Preheat oven to 350 degrees.
2. Cut croissants in half lengthwise and place the bottom halves on a baking sheet. Place tomato slices on croissant bottoms.
3. In a medium bowl, combine eggs, milk, salt and pepper to taste; beat well.
4. In a medium skillet, melt butter over medium heat. Add the egg mixture and scramble until firm but not browned.
5. Spoon the scrambled eggs onto the croissant bottoms. Place a piece of cheese on the eggs and replace the top of each croissant. Top each croissant with another piece of cheese.
6. Bake for 3-4 minutes or until heated through and the cheese is melted.

2724 WEST 4TH AVENUE, VANCOUVER, BC

NAAM

"Sharing food with another human being is an intimate act that should not be indulged in lightly."
M. F. K. Fisher

SWEET PERI-PERI CREME BRULEE WITH PERSIMMON SORBET

Nando's legend has come to life and is larger than life in some parts. It's a story that dates back to the start of humankind, where people gathered around the flame to share their life experiences. Nando's heritage is one seeped in legend, Portuguese-style cooking and the magic of Nando's secret ingredient, Peri-Peri.

Ingredients:
Brûleé:
1L cream
250g sugar
1 vanilla pod
1 tbsp. strained sweet peri-peri sauce
100g icing sugar

Persimmon Sorbet:
500g persimmon pulp
500g sugar
750 ml water
60 ml lemon juice
1 egg white

Instructions:
Brûleé:
1. Bring the cream and the vanilla pod to the boil.
2. Whisk together the egg yolks and sugar.
3. Pour over the boiling cream.
4. Whisk continuously on a low heat until thick.
5. Strain through a sieve.
6. Add Nando's sweet peri-peri sauce.
7. Cool in fridge.
8. Sprinkle with icing sugar and brûleé with blowtorch.

Persimmon Sorbet:
1. Bring fruit, sugar and water to the boil.
2. Blend with emersion blender.
3. Strain and cool.
4. Add lemon juice and egg white.
5. Freeze using sorbetiere.

NANDO'S FLAME-GRILLED CHICKEN

2064 WEST 41ST AVENUE, VANCOUVER, BC

"So long as you have food in your mouth, you have solved all questions for the time being."
Franz Kafka

Lemon, Cumin and Sumac Roasted Cauliflower

The concept is inspired by an independent and modern Beirut during the 1940's when it was an intellectual and cultural mecca; considered the Paris of the Middle East. The Nuba restaurant has a 60+seat capacity and a 26-foot bar. We now offer fresh pressed juices, fair trade organic coffee, and a wine list with a special focus on organic products that reflect the simplicity of our menu and our commitment to value. Our approach to beverages is no different than with our food; Nuba's cocktails are made from scratch with fresh fruit juices, organic ingredients and natrual sweeteners. It is possible to nurture your body even when you are having fun.

Ingredients:
I large head of cauliflower, broken into florets
⅓ c olive oil
1 large lemon, zested & juiced
1 tbsp. ground cumin
1 tbsp. ground sumac
1 tsp. garlic powder
1 large pinch kosher salt
good grind fresh black pepper
additional lemon, quartered (optional)

Instructions:

1. Preheat oven to 425F.

2. In a large bowl, combine the cauliflower, olive oil, lemon juice and zest, cumin, sumac and garlic powder.

3. Toss with your hands or a wooden spoon so that everything gets evenly combined.

4. Dump onto a cookie sheet prepped with a silpat mat or parchment paper and sprinkle with salt and pepper.

5. Bake for 30 minutes, flipping cauliflower over at the 15 minute mark. When everything is golden brown and crispy, remove from oven.

6. Serve with additional lemon quarters for that added lemony bite.

207 West Hastings Street, Vancouver, BC

NUBA

"I want to make lemonade out of the lemons that were dealt to me."
Baron Hill

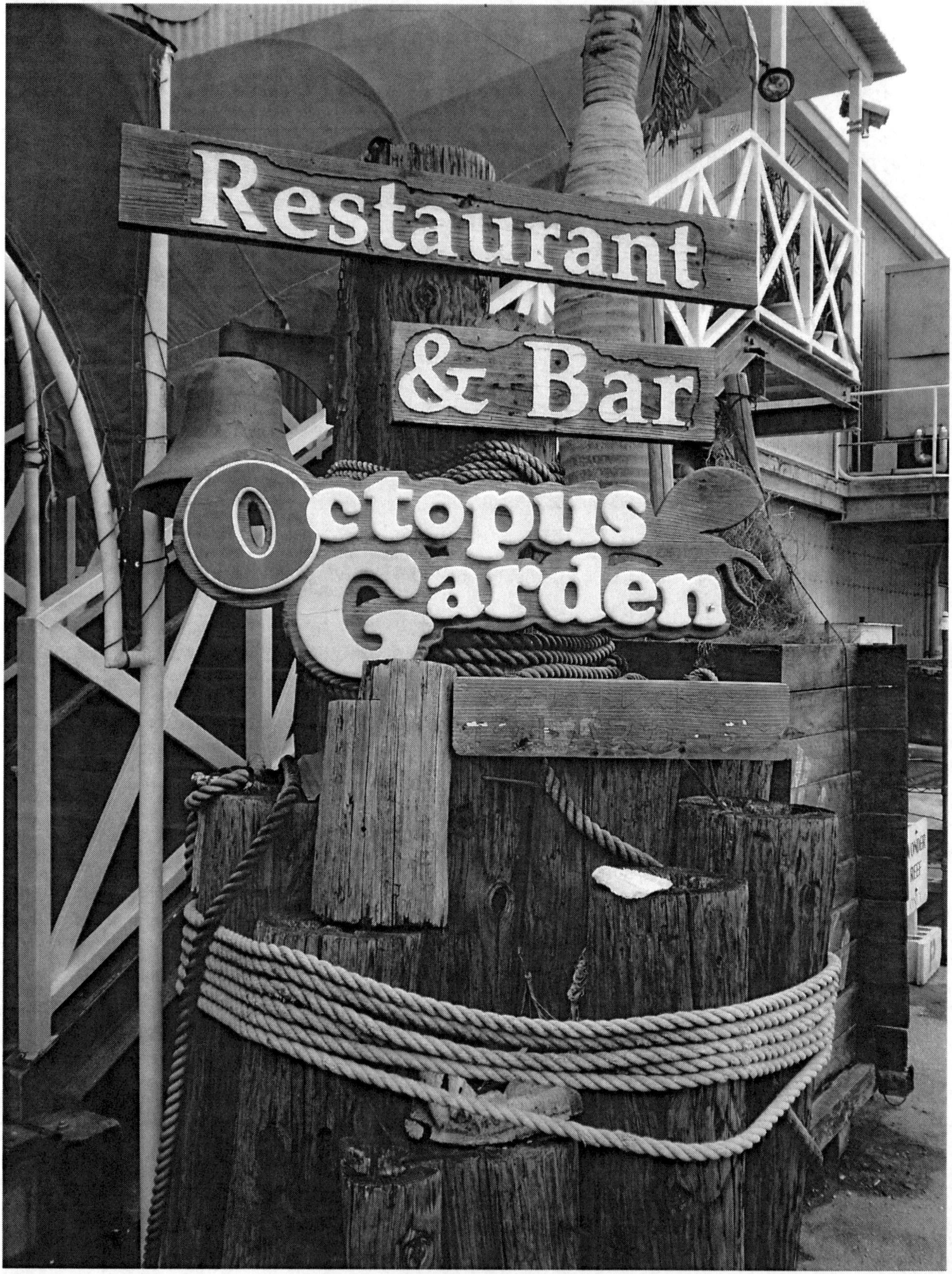
Restaurant
& Bar
Octopus
Garden

KAPPA MAKI ROLL

For many Japanese, it is a classic choice for traditional omakase. Food can influence anyone's mood and Octopus Garden works its magic better than Ursala from The Little Mermaid. This tiny Japanese restaurant has been around for twenty years, but it feels like its popularity has really taken off over the last few. They're most known for their omakase and sushi and it's certainly a neighbourhood gem and local favourite. From the outside, the restaurant looks quite large, but the space is small and the seating is tight. However the service is warm so it makes for a cozy atmosphere.

Ingredients:
3 C. of sushi rice, cooked
and cooled
1 cucumber
Nori, 6 to 7 sheets
salt
soy sauce or shoyu
wasabi paste

Instructions:
1. Wash the cucumber and peel it, if desired. Scoop out the seeds and discard them. Slice the cucumber lengthwise into thin sticks and sprinkle it with a dash of salt.

2. Lay the nori sheets on a bamboo mat or a flat surface and spread a thin layer of sushi rice over about ⅔ of the nori, leaving an edge closest to you uncovered. If necessary, dampen your fingers with vinegar water to spread the rice thinly and evenly.

OCTOPUS' GARDEN

1995 CORNWALL AVENUE, VANCOUVER, BC

"Statistics show that of those who contract the habit of eating, very few survive."
George Bernard Shaw

OPUS 97

Signature Tastes of VANCOUVER

The chic 'see-and-be-seen' OPUS Bar in world-renowned OPUS Hotel Vancouver, now boasts a new re-mix of eccentric furniture with an affluent disregard for style rules. The heat has been turned up with splashes of amplified pink, saturated lavendar, and a glow wall taking on the color of a chemical sunset - the perfect backdrop for Vancouver's style savvy crowd. Over lively conversation, innovative cocktails and an eclectic "O Bites" menu, enjoy live music from the city's best DJs. Glass-walled restrooms and live video feeds allow you to always keep an eye on the action and indulge your inner voyeurism. Located in fashionable Yaletown, OPUS Bar has been consistently voted "Vancouver's Most Popular Nightspot" by Zagat.

Ingredients:
45ml of Grey Goose l'orange,
15ml of Alize gold
30 ml of blood orange puree
30ml of passion fruit puree

Instructions:
1. All ingredients are combined in a shaker with ice shaken and then strained into a martini glass.

2. We garnish with a cape gooseberry.

350 DAVIE ST., VANCOUVER, BC

OPUS BAR

"That's a big goal of mine, to try and grow as much of my own food as possible."
Daryl Hannah

THAI CURED SALMON

A vibrant gathering place of celebration or an exclusive intimate dining experience for two; ORU is the perfect spot to savour food of the Pacific Northwest and flavours of the Pacific Rim. A marble and stainless steel open concept kitchen sets the stage upon which our innovative and talented chefs create extraordinary cuisine. Allow our dynamic and passionately-driven ORU team to guide you through a culinary journey for the senses with a menu that features a variety of dishes of local origin with a twist from the Pacific Rim, simply and skillfully prepared.

Ingredients:
1 stalk of lemongrass
½ oz. fresh peeled ginger
2 lime leaves, julienned
juice of 2 limes, plus extra for garnish
1 C. sugar
½ C. salt
5 oz. piece skinned sockeye salmon fillet
2 tbsp. grape seed oil
salt and white pepper
fish sauce (optional)

Instructions:

1. In a food processor, blend lemongrass, ginger, lime leaves, lime juice, sugar and salt.

2. Place mixture in a shallow dish, and put skinned fillet of salmon into the mixture so it comes halfway up the side of the sockeye salmon fillets, with the (formerly skin) side down. Cover and refrigerate for 8 hours.

3. Remove from refrigerator and pat dry.

4. Heat a frying pan on high for one minute, and then reduce to medium heat. Add grape seed oil and heat until the pan is slightly smoking.

5. Season fish with a sprinkle of salt and season both sides with ground white pepper. Carefully place fillet in oiled pan non-skinned side down. Do not touch the fish or shake the pan. Allow to sear for 4 minutes or until fish is cooked to medium. The cured half of fish is a great contrast to the beautifully seared side of salmon.

6. Serve with jasmine rice, vegetables, a squeeze of lime juice and a sprinkle of fish sauce.

ORU RESTAURANT
1038 CANADA PLACE, VANCOUVER, BC

"If I had the choice between smoked salmon and tinned salmon, I'd have it tinned. With vinegar."
Harold Wilson

ROYAL BERRY TORTE

Pacific Institute of Culinary Arts (PICA) is Vancouver's most progressive centre for culinary and baking & pastry arts education. Since 1997 our accredited Institute has offered highly regarded career programs in Culinary Arts and Baking & Pastry Arts with the option of expanding your career training with a 1-Year Culinary/Baking & Pastry Arts program. Our programs are 90% hands-on taught in guaranteed small class sizes and designed for students who wish to be productive immediately in a professional environment upon graduation.

Ingredients:
Chocolate Mousse:
4 eggs
3 oz. sugar 85 g.
8 oz. couverture/ chocolate coating 250 g.
3 sheets gelatin, soaked in water
2 tsp. rum 35 g.
2 pts., 1 oz. whipped cream (soft peaks, chilled) 650 ml.

Strawberry and Raspberry Mousse:
11 oz.pureed strawberries 400 g.
11 oz. pureed raspberries 350 g.
13 oz. sugar 400 g.
1 tsp. lemon juice 5 g.
8 sheets gelatin, soaked in water
1 pt., 3 oz. whipped cream (soft peeks, chilled) 400 g.
8 to 10 prepared profiterolles, depending on their size.
chocolate sponge cake

Instructions:
For the Chocolate Mousse:
1. Whip the eggs and sugar to a foam consistency.
2. Melt the chocolate, let cool slightly, then add to the egg and sugar foam.
3. Add the rum and gelatin and let cool even more. Fold in whipped cream.

For the Berry Mousse:
1. Bring the pureed strawberries and raspberries, sugar and lemon juice to a boil.
2. Add the gelatin and let cool. Fold the whipped cream into the cooled fruit mixture.
3. Fill prepared profiteroles (choux paste) with the Strawberry and Raspberry Mousse and freeze.
**These can be prepared in advance

To Assemble the Torte:
1. In advance, prepare a base of chocolate sponge cake using your favorite recipe and cut to fit inside a torte ring lined with an acetate strip.
2. Place 8 to 10 Strawberry and Raspberry Mousse-filled profiteroles on the sponge base, leaving the outside edges free.
3. Fill to the top of the ring with chocolate mousse, leveling off the top. Freeze.
4. Decorate the torte with chocolate ruffles and dust with cocoa powder and/or icing sugar.

"The food that enters the mind must be watched as closely as the food that enters the body."
Pat Buchanan

SEARED VENISON CRUSTED WITH GIN BOTANICALS AND SAUTÉED CABBAGE

A short 10 minute scenic drive from downtown Victoria is Paprika Bistro. Owned & operated by local resident and long time Restaurateur Geoff Parker, it is located in the heart of Oak Bay and only blocks from Willows Beach. Paprika is a 60 seat boutique restaurant with a locally inspired European menu and an international wine list with a great presence of BC wines. The menu & daily features offer seasonal cuisine showcasing the best Vancouver Island has to offer. Paprika has a private room that holds up to 20 guests or book out the whole restaurant for larger groups.

Ingredients:
10 oz venison loin (available with notice at Slater's Meats)
1 tsp. each: angelica, orris root, star anise, orange peel, lemon peel, cinnamon, rose petal
1 tbsp. each-juniper and coriander*
2 C. thinly sliced green cabbage
1 tbsp. butter
2 oz. Victoria gin
lemon

Instructions:

1. Grind all your botanicals together (coffee grinder works best) *some of these spices are harder to find then others, don't worry if you can't find them all, the juniper and coriander are the most important, use what you can find.

2. Season your venison with salt and pepper, then pack it in the botanical blend.

3. In a hot pan sear your crusted venison (for appetizers sear for about 10 seconds each side, for main course about a minute on each side) watching your heat so your botanicals don't burn.

4. Remove meat from the pan and allow to rest.

5. Sauté your cabbage in the butter and season with salt and pepper.

6. Once your cabbage is soft, deglaze with Victoria gin and reduce.

7. Add a small squeeze of lemon juice.

8. Slice your venison and serve on top of your cabbage for a main or slice very thin and wrap it around your cabbage securing it with a skewer for an appetizer.

9. Serves two as a main course or many for canapés. Suggested drink pairing: Apple Martini.

PAPRIKA BISTRO

2524 ESTEVAN AVE., VICTORIA, BC

"An idealist is one who, on noticing that roses smell better than a cabbage, concludes that it will also make better soup."
H. L. Mencken

Local revamped. Comfortable redefined. The Pear Tree Restaurant is a destination outside the mold, bringing together world-class cuisine and downtown elegance with approachability and a sense of community. With an emphasis on freshness and high quality, Chef Jaeger incorporates seasonal local, organic and sustainable ingredients to create a sublime year-round menu. Owned and operated by husband-and-wife team Scott and Stephanie Jaeger, The Pear Tree Restaurant is the destination whether it be a special occasion, catching up with friends, or a relaxed weekday dinner.

Ingredients:
300 g Hazelnut powder, fine
200g icing sugar
92.5 g egg whites, whipped frothy

Instructions:
1. Mix 92.5 g egg whites, whipped, 300 g sugar, and 100g water.

2. Cook sugar and water to 116 C slowly, add egg white.

3. Fold 1 and 2.

4. Bake at 285F for 17 to 20 minutes.

4120 HASTINGS ST. BURNABY, BC

PEAR TREE

"Good food ends with good talk."
Geoffrey Neighor

SALADE VERTE

A delightful neighbourhood bistro, Pied-â-Terre offers just thirty seats in a setting that celebrates simplicity. Crisp white walls accent rich black leather upholstered chairs, and an ornate black chandelier lights the room's opposing banquettes. This bijou restaurant is your new home away from home.

Ingredients:

For dressing:
1½ tbsp. tarragon vinegar
⅛ tsp. anisette or other anise-flavored liqueur (optional)
¼ tsp. Dijon mustard
2 tsp. finely chopped fresh parsley
2 tsp. finely chopped fresh tarragon
2 tsp. finely chopped fresh chervil
½ tsp. salt
⅛ tsp. black pepper
⅓ C. vegetable or olive oil

For Salad:
1 head romaine (1 lb.), ribs removed
½ head escarole (½ lb.)
¼ head iceberg lettuce (¼ lb.)
½ head Boston lettuce (2 oz.), ribs removed
1 Belgian endive, leaves separated and torn in half crosswise
1 (3-inch-long) heel from a day-old baguette
1 garlic clove, halved crosswise

Instructions:

Make Dressing:
1. Whisk together all dressing ingredients except oil in a small bowl.
2. Add oil in a slow stream, whisking constantly until dressing is emulsified.

Make Salad:
1. Tear romaine, escarole, iceberg, and Boston lettuce into bite-size pieces and toss with endive in a large salad bowl (preferably wooden).
2. Rub bread liberally all over with garlic and toss with greens.
3. Add dressing, toss well, then discard bread. Serve immediately.

3369 CAMBIE STREET, VANCOUVER, BC

PIED-À-TERRE

"I don't always prepare such rich meals. Sometimes I'll just serve a simple quiche, salad and dessert for dinner. During the week I try to eat lightly.
Paul Lynde

Pink Peppercorn
Seafood House

DINNER MENU

LOBSTER BISQUE

Signature Taste of VANCOUVER

The Pink Peppercorn Seafood House makes all events special and memorable with our fine dining style food that will cater to your high standards. "Our goal is to provide the best cuisine, service and décor to all of our customers, and we are dedicated to making great food accompanied with passion."

Ingredients:
16 C. water
1½ C. dry white wine
two 1¼ lb. live lobsters
¾ lb. large shrimp
(about 18), shelled,
reserving shells, and
deveined if desired
2 medium onions
1 fennel bulb, chopped
(about 2 C.), reserving
fronds for garnish if
desired
4 large carrots, chopped
1 celery rib, chopped
2 bay leaves
¾ tsp. dried thyme,
crumbled
¼ C. fresh parsley sprigs
¼ tsp. black peppercorns
the zest of 1 navel orange,
removed in strips with a
vegetable peeler
3 garlic cloves, minced
2 tbsp. olive oil
¼ tsp. saffron threads
a 28- to 32-oz. can
whole tomatoes,
drained and chopped
¼ C. heavy cream
1½ tbsp. Pernod, or to
taste
1 tbsp. fresh lemon
juice, or to taste

Instructions:
1. In a large (5-to 6-quart) kettle combine water and 1 cup wine and bring to a boil. Plunge lobsters into liquid head-first and return liquid to a boil. Simmer lobsters, covered, 9 minutes. With tongs plunge lobsters immediately into cold water to stop cooking, reserving cooking liquid.
2. Working over a bowl to catch the juices, twist off tails and claws and reserve juices. Discard tomalley, head sacs, and any roe and remove meat from tails and claws, reserving it separately.
3. To reserved cooking liquid add lobster shells, reserved lobster juices and shrimp shells, 1 onion, quartered, 1 cup fennel, half of carrots, celery, 1 bay leaf, thyme, parsley, peppercorns, and zest. Simmer mixture gently, uncovered, skimming froth occasionally, 1 1/4 hours.
4. Strain stock through a large sieve set over a large bowl and pour into cleaned kettle. Boil stock until reduced to about 6 cups and return to bowl. Stock, cooked lobster, and shelled raw shrimp keep, covered separately and chilled, 1 day.
5. In a kettle cook remaining onion, chopped fine, remaining 1 cup fennel, remaining carrots, remaining bay leaf, garlic, and salt and pepper to taste in oil over moderate heat, stirring, until vegetables are softened.
6. Add remaining ½ cup wine and boil until mostly evaporated. Add saffron, tomatoes, and shellfish stock and simmer, covered, 20 minutes. Add shrimp and reserved lobster claw meat (reserving tail meat) and simmer 2 minutes, or until shrimp are cooked through. Remove soup from heat and remove 6 shrimp, reserving them. Discard bay leaf.
7. In a blender purée soup in batches until smooth, transferring as it is puréed to a very fine sieve set over a saucepan. Force soup through sieve, pressing hard on solids, and whisk in cream, Pernod, and salt and pepper to taste. Heat bisque over moderate heat until hot (do not boil) and stir in lemon juice.
8. Chop fine reserved shrimp and lobster tail meat and divide among heated soup bowls. Ladle soup over shellfish and garnish with reserved fennel fronds.

PINK PEPPERCORN SEAFOOD
1485 KINGSWAY. VANCOUVER, BC

"Hey, we all have our fear. Mine is bugs and lobsters!"
Brooke Burke

HABAÑERO DUSTED AHI TUNA WITH AVOCADO & MANGO SALAD

Signature Tastes of VANCOUVER

Located in the Yaletown district of downtown Vancouver where Davie Street meets False Creek; Provence Marinaside is a great place to meet your friends on the patio or at our bar. Watch the action in the marina or on the seawall. Our award winning food, warm ambiance, and friendly service turns every meal into a special occasion. Fresh local seafood; raw oyster bar; antipasti showcase; extensive wine list; private room; take-out; gourmet picnic baskets. A visit to Provence transports you to the South of France without the jetlag.

Ingredients:
5 oz. portion of Ahi tuna
½ tsp. dried habañero
½ sliced avocado
½ sliced mango
1 tbsp. shredded coconut (toasted)
1 tbsp. chopped fresh cilantro
1 lime (halved)
1½ tbsp. olive oil
1 tbsp. salt

Instructions:

1. Heat pan on high heat then add olive oil.

2. Season the tuna with sea salt & habañero.

3. Lightly sear tuna on all sides & remove from pan.

4. Gently toss the avocado and mango with fresh lime juice, olive oil & sea salt.

5. Arrange avocado and mango salad on a plate.

6. Slice tuna and fan over salad.

7. Garnish with cilantro, coconut and fresh lime juice.

8. Finish with a pinch of sea salt on the tuna.

PROVENCE MARINASIDE

1177 MARINASIDE CRESCENT, VANCOUVER, BC

"Love, like a chicken salad or restaurant hash, must be taken with blind faith or it loses its flavor."
Helen Rowland

MESCLUN GREEN SALAD

Jean Francis and Alessandra Quaglia, both chefs, met in France while brushing shoulders in the kitchen of several hotels. Romance and marriage followed soon after.They worked together again in Vancouver at the Wall Center Hotel. In December 1997 they bravely embarked upon a project called Provence Mediterranean Grill. With its cozy neighbourhood feel, this Point Grey restaurant enjoys enormous success, with a loyal local following. The restaurant won Gold for Best Bistro in the 2002 Vancouver Magazine Restaurant Awards. Building on their success, and wishing to share their love of French/Italian cuisine in a comfortable atmosphere, they bring you Provence Marinaside on Vancouver's trendy Yaletown waterfront.

Ingredients:
16 asparagus spears, pencil size
6 oz. package Mesclun greens

Fava Bean Crostini:
3½ lbs. fresh fava beans, shelled (4 C.)
2 garlic cloves, smashed
2 tsp. finely chopped thyme
2 tsp. fresh lemon juice
1 tsp. finely grated lemon zest
1 C. extra-virgin olive oil, plus more for drizzling
salt and freshly ground pepper
twenty-four ½-in.-thick slices of Italian bread
lemon wedges, for serving

Instructions:
1. Trim asparagus spears to 4-inches long, steam until tender crisp; plunge into an ice bath, drain well and toss with a small amount of lemon vinaigrette dressing (recipe below). Arrange 8 asparagus spears on each plate in 'Lincoln log' squares.
2. Drizzle Mesclun greens with dressing, place inside the Lincoln log squares, garnish plate with a small amount of dressing around the asparagus and serve this beautiful mesclun salad.

Fava Bean Crostini:
3. Preheat the broiler. Bring a medium saucepan of water to a boil. Add the beans and cook until tender, about 5 minutes. Drain the beans and transfer to a bowl of ice water to cool. Drain, then peel and discard the tough outer skins.
4. In a food processor, puree the beans with the garlic, thyme, lemon juice and lemon zest. With the machine on, add ¾ cup of the olive oil in a thin stream and process until smooth. Scrape the fava bean puree into a medium bowl and season with salt and pepper.
5. Brush the bread slices on both sides with the remaining ¼ cup of olive oil. Arrange the slices on a baking sheet and broil about 4 inches from the heat for 1 minute per side, or until golden and crisp.
6. Spread the toasts with the fava bean puree and arrange the crostini on a platter. Drizzle with olive oil, sprinkle with salt and serve with lemon wedges.

PROVENCE MEDITERRANEAN GRILL
4473 W 10TH AVE, VANCOUVER, BC

"What garlic is to salad, insanity is to art."
Augustus Saint-Gaudens

SALSICCIA

(Vancouver, BC) December 10, 2010 – Q4 al Centro, the sister restaurant to the ever-popular Q4 Ristorante in Kitsilano, opens for its first dinner service at 5pm on Friday, December 10. Q4 al Centro will be open for dinner nightly, Monday through Saturday, from 5pm, and lunch Monday to Friday from 11:30am. Q4 al Centro is located at 780 Richards Street in the heart of Vancouver's entertainment district. Reservations are recommended, please phone 604.687.4444.

Signature Taste of VANCOUVER

Ingredients:
200 ml. bought aïoli (I use Food by Chefs Free-Range Egg Aïoli)
2 tbsp. wholegrain mustard
3 gherkins, finely diced
2 tbsp. capers
1 tbsp. chopped parsley
salt and freshly ground black pepper
4 medium all-purpose potatoes, peeled and diced 3 cm.
3 carrots, peeled and sliced 2 cm. thick
1 L chicken stock
1 fresh bay leaf
6 good-quality pure pork sausages (about 800 g.)
250 g. green beans, stalk ends cut off and beans halved
4 spring onions, root ends trimmed and green leaf cut off

Instructions:

1. Put the aïoli, mustard, gherkins, capers and parsley in a bowl, and mix well. Taste and season. Reserve.

2. Put the potatoes and carrots, stock and bay leaf in a saucepan. Bring to the boil and simmer for 5 minutes then add the sausages and simmer for 10-15 minutes until the sausages are cooked.

3. Remove the sausages. Add the beans and spring onions, and simmer a further 5 minutes until everything is tender. Taste and season.

4. Slice the sausages and serve with the vegetables and a little broth with a dollop of the aïoli.

780 RICHARDS STREET, VANCOUVER, BC

Q4 AL CENTRO

"The less food, the more time to talk, the more to talk about."
Damon Wayans

207

CRISPY ARANCINI

Ingredients:
1L (4 C.) chicken stock
1 tbsp. olive oil
1 brown onion, finely chopped
2 garlic cloves, crushed
330 g. (1½ C.) arborio rice
40 g. (½ C.) shredded parmesan
4 eggs
180 g. (2 C.) dried (packaged) breadcrumbs
150 g. (1 C.) plain flour
100 g. mozzarella, cut into 1.5cm pieces
vegetable oil, to deep-fry
tomato relish or chutney, to serve
bought marinated olives, to serve
bought marinated feta, to serve

Instructions:
1. Place the stock in a medium saucepan over high heat and bring just to the boil. Cover and reduce heat to low. Hold at a gentle simmer.
2. Meanwhile, heat the oil in a large saucepan over medium heat. Add the onion and garlic and cook, covered, stirring occasionally, for 5 minutes or until the onion is soft.
3. Add the rice to the onion mixture and cook, stirring, until the grains appear slightly glassy. Add a ladleful (about 125ml/½ cup) of the simmering stock to the rice mixture and stir constantly with a wooden spoon until the liquid is completely absorbed. Continue to add the stock, 1 ladleful at a time, stirring constantly and allowing the liquid to be absorbed before adding the next ladleful, for 20 minutes or until the rice is tender yet firm to the bite and the risotto is creamy. Stir in the parmesan. Set aside for 2-3 hours to cool completely. Add 2 eggs and stir until well combined.
4. Place the breadcrumbs on a large plate. Place the flour in a bowl. Crack the remaining eggs into a separate bowl and use a fork to lightly whisk. Use wet hands to shape 2 tablespoons of the risotto mixture into a ball. Press your thumbs into the centre of the ball to make an indent. Place a piece of mozzarella in the indent, then mould the risotto mixture around the mozzarella to enclose. Repeat with the remaining risotto mixture and mozzarella to make 28 balls.
5. Roll the risotto balls in the flour and shake off any excess. Dip in the egg, then in the breadcrumbs, pressing to coat. Place on a large plate. Place in the fridge for 30 minutes to chill.
6. Add enough oil in a large saucepan to reach a depth of 5cm. Heat to 190°C over medium-high heat (when the oil is ready a cube of bread will turn golden in 10 seconds). Add 7 risotto balls to the oil and cook, turning occasionally, for 4-5 minutes or until golden. Use a slotted spoon to transfer to a plate lined with paper towel. Repeat, in 3 more batches, with the remaining risotto balls, reheating the oil between batches.
7. Place the risotto balls on a serving plate and serve with tomato chutney and marinated olives and feta.

Signature Tastes of VANCOUVER

2611 WEST 4TH AVENUE, VANCOUVER, BC

Q4 RISTORANTE

"The most remarkable thing about my mother is that for thirty years she served the family nothing but leftovers. The original meal has never been found."
Calvin Trillin

Yogurt Honey Sorbet Macerated Blueberries Jelly Mead

Raincity Grill opened it's doors in 1992, featuring a menu comprised of locally sourced food, eventually incorporating what became our trademark 100-Mile Tasting Menu. The ingredients represent a commitment to both the present and the future, by providing you with products that are raised, grown, and caught in the most ethical manner available. Our menu is a tribute to the local farmers, fisherman and producers of British Columbia. The Chef sources out the best organic, sustainable products available and has designed a menu to showcase the individual components by blending them into a harmony of world-class flavors. "Farm-to-table" has become a recent catch phrase but at Raincity Grill it has been a philosophy for twenty years.

Ingredients:
4½ C. plain whole-milk yogurt, plus a little more for plating
1 C. plus 3½ tsp. honey
1½ C. whole milk
1 C. blueberries
1¼ C. mead
2 sheets gelatin

Instructions:
To Make Sorbet:
1. Bring yogurt, 1 cup honey and milk to a simmer over low heat. Strain and chill mixture for a minimum of 2 hours (overnight is better).
2. Churn in ice-cream maker, freeze.

To Make Macerated Blueberries:
1. Combine berries and 3½ teaspoons honey; reserve in fridge for about 30 minutes.

To Make Jelly of Mead:
1. Place mead in a small pan and bring to a simmer; carefully light mead to burn off alcohol.
2. Rehydrate gelatin sheets by soaking briefly in water.
3. Add rehydrated gelatin to warm mead, strain and chill for 3 to 5 hours.

To Finish:
1. Chill 8 plates.
2. Take some yogurt and draw a pleasing pattern on the plates. Place 2 scoops of sorbet on each plate, then evenly divide the berries and jelly of mead. Finish the plates with some of the liquid extracted from the berries.

1193 DENMAN STREET, VANCOUVER, BC

RAINCITY GRILL

"We may find in the long run that tinned food is a deadlier weapon than the machine-gun."
George Orwell

RICKARD'S DARK BEER TURKEY DINNER

At Rickard's, we're all about a friendly invitation into the flavourful world of beer. We are proud to have the #1 Red, #1 White and #1 Dark (Porter) beers in Canada and have most recently introduced Rickard's Blonde, a truly flavourful yet refreshing Pilsner, into our family. Try pairing a Rickard's with your next meal and see what different flavour combinations you can unlock!

Ingredients:

Turkey:
1 whole 8 lb Turkey
1/3 C. of Cajun seasoning
1 tall boy can Rickard's Dark
1/4 C. salt and pepper
1/4 C. vegetable oil

Gravy:
1 bottle Rickard's Dark
10 to 12 bacon strips, chopped
2 C. white onions, chopped
2 tbsp. maple syrup
1 tsp. ground pepper
2 C. turkey pan drippings
2 tbsp. malt vinegar
2 tbsp. flour

Cranberry Stuffing:
4 oz. Rickard's Dark
14 oz. seasoned bread crumbs
1 C. dried cranberries
1 C. butter
2 large white onions, chopped
3 stalks celery, chopped
2 garlic cloves, peeled and smashed
1 lb. pork sausage
2 eggs
1 tbsp. dried parsley flakes
1 tbsp. paprika
1 tbsp. sage
1 tsp. rosemary
4 C. chicken stock
2 tbsp. flour

Instructions:

Turkey:
1. Remove neck and giblets. Roast to use with gravy.
2. Rinse turkey inside and out then pat dry with paper towels.
3. Rub the turkey lightly with oil and rub inside and out with salt, pepper and the Cajun seasoning. Set aside.
4. Preheat barbecue on high. Open your Rickard's Dark and place beer can on a solid surface.
5. Grabbing a turkey leg in each hand, plunk the bird 'cavity' over the beer can.
6. Turn one side of the burner completely off and the other side a medium-high heat.
7. Place the turkey stuffed with the Rickard's Dark can on the side that is turned off to apply the indirect cooking method.
8. Place the bird on its two legs with the can and gently balance the turkey on the grill.
9. Close the lid to grill over medium indirect heat for approximately 1¼ hours or until the internal temperature reaches 170 degrees F (77 degrees C) in the breast area and 180 degrees F (83 degrees C) in the thickest part of the thigh.
10. In a saucepan, carefully remove from grill and let rest for 12-15 minutes before removing the Rickard's Dark can. Be careful not to spill, contents will be hot. Carve turkey and serve immediately.

Gravy:
1. Using a skillet or sauté pan, fry the chopped bacon until crispy.
2. Using turkey drippings; pour 2 cups of the degreased drippings into a saucepan and then reduce to about one-half over high heat.
3. Turn heat to medium and stir in chopped onions; simmer for about 10 minutes.
4. Stir in remaining ingredients (except beer and flour) and cook for about 10 minutes.
5. Deglaze with beer and reduce for another 10 to 15 minutes over high heat.
6. Place pan in ice-water bath to cool a bit.
7. When lukewarm, purée gravy in blender and strain through sieve.
8. Return gravy to pan and reheat over medium burner.
9. Stir in flour and cook for 3 to 4 minutes, stirring constantly, until gravy thickens.

Cranberry Stuffing:
1. Melt the butter in a saucepan.
2. Sauté onions, celery and garlic until lightly browned. Remove and set aside.
3. Without rinsing pan, add sausage and cook until lightly browned.
4. In large bowl, combine seasoned bread crumbs, cranberries, sautéed onions, celery, garlic, and sausage mixture. Combine thoroughly.
5. Add eggs, parsley, paprika, sage, rosemary and 1 cup of chicken stock.
6. You may wish to hand-mix to assure thorough blending of ingredients.
7. Add more chicken stock until dressing sticks together firmly.
8. Place the mixture either inside your turkey or in a lightly greased casserole dish and bake at 350 for 18 minutes.

"A lot of Thanksgiving days have been ruined by not carving the turkey in the kitchen."
Kin Hubbard

COCO CURRY SHRIMP

Signature Tastes of VANCOUVER

Ingredients:
1 (14-oz.) can unsweetened coconut milk (not low-fat)
1 tbsp. fresh lime juice
1 tbsp. curry powder
2 tsps. minced ginger
salt and freshly ground black pepper
1 lb. large shrimp, peeled and deveined
lime wedges, for serving

Instructions:

1. In a large pot whisk together the coconut milk, lime juice, curry powder and ginger. Slowly bring to a low boil over low heat.

2. Simmer for until slightly reduced and thickened, about 7 to 10 minutes.

3. Taste for seasoning and add salt and or pepper, if needed.

4. Add the shrimp and simmer, covered, until the shrimp are fully cooked, about 12 to 15 minutes.

5. Transfer the curry to a serving bowl and serve with lime wedges.

RODNEY'S OYSTER HOUSE
1228 HAMILTON STREET, VANCOUVER, BC

"I shall be but a shrimp of an author."
Thomas Gray

Saffron indian cuisine

4300/5

OPEN

CUSTOMER PARKING AT REAR
UNDERGROUND PARKING LOT

WARNING

ALOO TIKKI

Signature Tastes of VANCOUVER

Ingredients:
500 g potatoes
2 slices white bread, medium size
1 medium onion, peeled and quartered
2-3 green chillies, stalk removed
1 in. piece of ginger, peeled
a small bunch of green coriander leaves finely chopped
salt to taste
½ tsp. Garam Masala
1 tsp. roast cumin powder
1 C. of oil for shallow frying

Instructions:
1. Boil potatoes in their skin, until soft. I cook them in pressure cooker for 4-5 minutes or microwave in a plastic bag, with 2-3 tbsp. water, for 8 minutes.
2. Cool, peel and mash potatoes. You can grate them coarsely. They do not need to be too smooth.
3. Chop finely or process onions, ginger, green chillies.
4. Chop bread slices finely in a food processor, to make crumbs. They should not be ground to a paste. Slightly 'rough texture' of ingredients adds to the taste.
5. Add crumbs, chopped coriander leaves, salt, garam masala and roast cumin powder to the boiled potatoes.
6. With oiled hands, divide it into 10-12 equal portions, roll them into balls and then flatten them into 'tikki' or burger shapes.
7. Heat 2-3 tbsp. of oil in a heavy bottomed frying pan. I use a non-stick pan, and fry 3-4 tikkies at a time, on medium heat, until nicely brown and crisp on both sides. You may need to add more oil for subsequent batches. They can be cooked up to this stage in advance.
8. When ready to serve, press each tikki with a flat spatula, squashing it flatter and cook it a little more, so more of it's surface gets crisp. A finished and properly squashed tikki does not have smooth edge.
9. Take out and place on absorbent paper.
10. Serve hot, with Imli Chutney and Green Mango Chutney.

NOTE: Another serving suggestion. You can make small tikkies, place them on a platter, top each with a tiny amount of finely chopped onions and tomatoes, then spoon 1 tsp. of Tamarind chutney on top and serve as finger food at a party.

SAFFRON INDIAN CUISINE
4300 KINGSWAY #5, BURNABY, BC

"We provide food that customers love, day after day after day. People just want more of it."
Ray Kroc

Salmon n' Bannock is a small cozy bistro with seats for about 25-30 people. It was tastefully decorated with many First Nations paintings adorning the wall. There are dream catchers and even a real canoe hanging from the ceiling! The menu is light and at a glance the prices are set quite reasonably.

Ingredients
4 C. of flour
½ tsp. of salt
1½ C. of sugar
4 C. of water
⅓ C. of baking powder
cooking oil

Instructions:

1. Combine dry ingredients.

2. Add half of the water.

3. Slowly add the rest of the liquid to completely moisten but not saturate flour mixture.

4. Let it rest for two to five minutes.

5. Shape and fry in shallow oil (¼-inch deep in the pot) until it's golden brown on each side.

SALMON 'N' BANNOCK BISTRO'S

1128 WEST BROADWAY, VANCOUVER, BC

"When baking, follow directions. When cooking, go by your own taste."
Laiko Bahrs

BROCCOLINI SAUTE

It all began on October 6, 1976 with the idea that an incredible view should be accompanied by great food in a unique setting. Hence, Salmon House on the Hill was born. The location alone set The Salmon House apart from anything else; no other commercial establishment was above Highway 1 and no other restaurant could boast the incredible scenery and view. The view from the dining room was something special that drew people through the doors from the start.

Ingredients:
1-4 tbsp. olive oil
1-2 tsp. crushed garlic
4 C. broccoli florets
salt
fresh ground black
pepper

Instructions:
1. Heat the olive oil in a 10" skillet over medium-low heat.

2. Add the garlic and cook for 1 minute.

3. Add the broccoli, salt and pepper and toss with the olive oil and garlic until the broccoli turns bright green and becomes tender.

4. Remove from the skillet and serve.

SALMON HOUSE ON THE HILL
2229 FOLKESTONE WAY, WEST VANCOUVER, BC

"When I eat with my friends, it is a moment of real pleasure, when I really enjoy my life."
Monica Bellucci

GRILLED CHEESE SANDWICH

Salt is a tasting room specializing in artisanal cheese, small-batch cured meats, and a dynamic array of wines, beers and sherries. Our menu is simple. Guests assemble a Tasting Plate from our chalkboard's selection of 10 cheeses, 10 meats, and 10 condiments. The selections change constantly, making it almost impossible to have the same Salt experience twice.

Ingredients:
4 slices white bread
3 tbsp. butter, divided
2 slices cheddar/artisan cheese

Instructions:
1. Preheat skillet over medium heat.

2. Generously butter one side of a slice of bread. Place bread butter-side-down onto skillet bottom and add 1 slice of cheese. Butter a second slice of bread on one side and place butter-side-up on top of sandwich.

3. Grill until lightly browned and flip over; continue grilling until cheese is melted.

4. Repeat with remaining 2 slices of bread, butter and slice of cheese.

SALT TASTING ROOM
45 BLOOD ALLEY, VANCOUVER, BC

"In the family sandwich, the older people and the younger ones can recognize one another as the bread. Those in the middle are, for a time, the meat."
Anna Quindlen

CHICKEN AND CHORIZO SALAD

Signature Tastes of VANCOUVER

Flickering candles. Mysterious belly dancers. Sexy and exotic Sanafir comes alive once the lights are dimmed. This is a room like no other in Vancouver. Join us at the bar, in the dining room or on one of our dining beds, for the epitome of decadent dining.

Ingredients:
6 chicken thighs
4 oz. red wine vinegar
2 chorizo sausages
2 white onions
¼ lb. spinach
¼ lb. arugula
2 large eggs

Paprika Aioli:
1 tbsp. grainy dijon
1 tbsp. brown sugar
3 cloves roasted garlic
1.5 tbsp. paprika
2 egg yolk
1 C. canola oil
1 oz. lime juice

Instructions:
Vinaigrette:
1. In a blender place the following: red wine vinegar, grainy dijon, brown sugar, lime juice, egg yolks, paprika, and roast garlic.
2. Begin blending, while all ingredients are blending, add canola oil into mixture slowly allowing it to emulsify all ingredients.
3. Season with salt to taste if necessary.

Salad:
1. In a large salad bowl add spinach and arugula and hard boiled eggs (boil eggs for 5 minutes).
2. Grill or bbq chicken thighs and chorizo.
3. When cooked cut to desired size.
4. Chop white onion and sweat in a pan until well caramelized.
5. Add thighs, chorizo and caramelized onion to salad bowl, toss with paprika aioli and enjoy.

1026 GRANVILLE STREET, VANCOUVER, BC

SANAFIR

"Sticking feathers up your butt does not make you a chicken."
Chuck Palahniuk

PRAWN COCKTAIL

Poised in Queen Elizabeth Park at the highest point in the city, and overlooking the exquisite quarry gardens, Seasons in the Park Restaurant is a local landmark in a class of its own, having set the standard for distinctive regional cuisine and exceptional service in Vancouver for almost 20 years. Centrally located and just a 10-minute drive from the Vancouver International Airport and Vancouver's downtown core, this glass-wrapped restaurant features stunning views of Vancouver's shimmering city skyline, the North Shore Mountains and Pacific Ocean. With innovative, seasonal dishes conceived by executive chef Dennis Peckham, the menu highlights West Coast and Pacific Rim influences and delivers clean, fresh, simple dishes.

Ingredients:
1 iceberg lettuce, washed, shredded
600g cooked school prawns, peeled

Cocktail Sauce:
60 ml. (¼ C.) tomato sauce
60 ml. (¼ C.) thin cream
1 tbsp. fresh lemon juice
1 tsp. worcestershire sauce
dash of red tabasco pepper sauce
salt & freshly ground black pepper

Instructions:
1. To make the cocktail sauce, combine the tomato sauce, cream, lemon juice, Worcestershire sauce and Tabasco in a small bowl. Taste and season with salt and pepper.

2. Place the lettuce in 4 serving dishes/glasses. Top with the prawns and drizzle with the cocktail sauce. Serve immediately.

CAMBIE & 33RD AVENUE QUEEN ELIZABETH PARK, VANCOUVER, BC

SEASONS IN THE PARK

"The key to everything is patience. You get the chicken by hatching the egg, not by smashing it."
Arnold H. Glasow

FRESH TOMATO SOUP

Signature Tastes of VANCOUVER

Ingredients:
2 tbsp. olive oil
1 onion, diced
2 cloves garlic, minced
6 beefsteak tomatoes, seeded and chopped
4 ripe Roma tomatoes, chopped
1 tsp. salt
⅛ tsp. white pepper
2 C. chicken or vegetable stock
2 tbsp. butter
2 tbsp. flour
½ tsp. orange zest
1 tbsp. minced fresh basil leaves
1 tsp. fresh thyme leaves

Instructions:
1. In heavy saucepan, heat oil and cook onions and garlic until tender. Add tomatoes, salt, pepper, and stock, and simmer for 20 minutes. Strain soup through a fine strainer.

2. In clean saucepan, melt butter and add flour; cook and stir for 2-3 minutes. Add ½ cup of the tomato mixture; cook and stir until thickened. Add remaining tomato mixture and cook and stir with wire whisk until mixture is hot and slightly thickened. Stir in orange zest, basil, and thyme leaves, and serve.

SECRET GARDEN TEA COMPANY
5559 WEST BOULEVARD, VANCOUVER, BC

"Good manners: The noise you don't make when you're eating soup.
Bennett Cerf

TAKO NO SUNOMONO

Signature Tastes of VANCOUVER

Ingredients:
¼ lb. boiled tako (sliced)
3 small cucumbers (or 1 large cucumber)
⅓ C. dried wakame (seaweed)
2 oz thinly cut ginger (optional)

Spices:
2 tbsp. vinegar
½ tsp. soy sauce
1½ tbsp. sugar
¼ tsp salt
1 tbsp. salt (for cucumber)

Instructions:
1. Peel the cucumber, then sprinkle salt on top and massage.

2. Rinse cucumber, pat dry, and slice into thin wheels.

3. Soak dried wakame (seaweed) in hot water a minute or so until it is moist.

4. Mix spices (vinegar, sugar, soy sauce and salt) in a small bowl.

5. Toss tako, cucumber, and wakame in a different bowl, then splash with mixed spices.

6. Place in a serving dish, top with ginger (optional), then chill in fridge before serving (optional, but recommended).

SETO JAPANESE RESTAURANT
8460 ALEXANDRA ROAD #155, RICHMOND, BC

"But I love fish, cheese and meat, and I eat everything, but only in small quantities if it's rich."
Eva Herzigova

CALABRESE PESTO

Opened in July 2000, Showcase has been known for its outstanding quality, innovative presentation and exceptional services. Join us and taste our extensive menu hand crafted by Chef Frank Gort. Watch a game and enjoy one of our local beers on tap, a glass of wine, and a bite to share. Enjoy sitting and people watching through our 15-foot windows, while one of our bartenders builds a cocktail made just for you. Showcase Bar is a great place to start the night or end your day.

Ingredients:
2 tbsp. dijon
3 cloves garlic
2 filets anchovies
1 tbsp. sambal
½ bunch mint
1 bunch parsley, curly
1.5 bunch basil
150 ml olive oil
75 g capers, finely chopped

Instructions:
1. Blend dijon, garlic, anchovies, sambal and olive oil until smooth.

2. Add the herbs one at a time in the order of mint, then parsley, then basil.

3. Make sure each herb is fully incorporated before adding more.

4. Add more olive oil if necessary.

5. Once all herbs are pureed, add the chopped capers & transfer to solo containers.

6. Final product should be thick & smooth, other than the bits of capers.

7. Try it with seared New Zeland Bream, warm fingerling potato salad and braised leaks.

Signature Taste of VANCOUVER

SHOWCASE RESTAURANT AND BAR
1122 WEST HASTINGS STREET, VANCOUVER, BC

"You don't need a silver fork to eat good food."
Paul Prudhomme

BBQ Sauce for Ribs

Inspired by our favorite nightspots in LA and New York, Society delivers quirky comfort food in style. From milkshakes with a kick, to the best burgers in town, there's something here you'll talk about for days after dinner. Imagine dimly lit booths filled with shadows cast by epic pink chandeliers. To be seen, or to hide away, both are possible, and pretty much anything goes. This is Society.

Ingredients:
2 jumbo onions
5 oz. bourbon
1 L of coffee
200 ml of honey
200 ml of crushed plum tomatoes
300ml of ketchup
500ml of veal stock
100 ml Worcestershire
40 ml tabasco

Instructions:

1. Slice the onion and caramelize them.

2. Deglaze with the bourbon.

3. Add all the liquids (coffe, veal stock, Tabasco, Worcestershire, ketchup, honey, bbq sauce).

4. Simmer until you get a thickened glaze consistency.

5. You can use this on any kind of meat, such as steak, beef ribs and pork ribs

SOCIETY DINING LOUNGE
1257 Hamilton Street, Vancouver, BC

"My first outdoor cooking memories are full of erratic British summers, Dad swearing at a barbecue that he couldn't put together, and eventually eating charred sausages, feeling brilliant."
Jamie Oliver

POPCORN ROCK SHRIMP

On behalf of all of the employees of Steamworks Brewing Company I am delighted to personally welcome you to our establishment. Since we first opened in 1995, Steamworks has been a favourite of Vancouver locals and visitors alike. Whether you're joining us for lunch, a drink after work, or a group dinner with friends and colleagues, we're honoured to have you with us.

Ingredients:
Spicy Honey:
1 C. honey
1 clove garlic, mashed
1 tbsp. peppercorn
1 tbsp. chili flakes
1 tbsp. smoked paprika
sea salt

Popcorn Shrimp:
Oil for deep-frying
2 C. of cornstarch
(Recommended: Maizena)
½ C. flour
salt and freshly ground
pepper
4 eggs, beaten
2 lbs. of rock shrimp

Garnish:
lemon wedges

Instructions:

1. Chuck Hughes' golden popcorn rock shrimp served with spicy honey are the perfect game day appetizer

2. For the spicy honey: In a saucepan, on medium heat, bring the honey, garlic, peppercorn, chili flakes, smoked paprika, and salt to a boil and let simmer for 2 minutes. Let cool, strain and transfer to a squeezable bottle. Keep aside.

3. For the popcorn shrimp: Preheat the deep-fat fryer to 360 degrees F.

4. In a bowl, mix together the cornstarch, flour, salt and pepper. Place the eggs in a bowl add the shrimp and coat. Remove the shrimp, letting the excess egg drip back into the bowl, then add the shrimp to the corn-starch mixture. Gently add to the fryer, turning until golden. Drain on paper towels and season with salt and pepper.

5. Serve immediately after frying and drizzle with the spicy honey and garnish with lemon wedges.

6. Keep the whirlpool going with the whisk as you slowly pour the egg mixture in the boiling broth.

7. Use the whisk to "scramble" the broth. After a few minutes stop whisking and you will see little shreds in the broth (hence the name "stracciatella" which comes from the Italian verb "stracciare" which means "to shred"

8. Serve with additional parmesan cheese if desired.

Signature Tastes of VANCOUVER

STEAMWORKS BREWING COMPANY
375 WATER STREET, VANCOUVER, BC

"Sitting down to a meal with an Indian family is different from sitting down to a meal with a British family."
Roland Joffe

新瑞華

SUN SUI WAH SEAFOOD RESTA

OPEN

RED BEAN SOUP WITH LOTUS SEED

The legend of Sun Sui Wah started over 30 years ago by it's founder in Sha Tin, Hong Kong. Based on the motto of "warm hospitality, superb quality and value!" it quickly joined the ranks of most popular dine out places and garnered high regard within the dining community. The "roasted squab" became a signature dish was famed throughout Hong Kong.

Signature Taste of VANCOUVER

3888 MAIN STREET, VANCOUVER, BC

SUN SUI

Ingredients:
300 g. red bean
50 g. lotus seed
50 g. Chinese lily bulb
25 g. rice grain/
glutinous rice
**Sun dried Mandarin
orange peel (one orange)**
200 g. sugar (add more
to adjust to your own
sweetness level)
5 pandan leaves
(screwpine leaves –
bundle up)
water

Instructions:
1. Get a 5L pot and fill up ³/₅ of the pot with water.
2. Wash the beans and rice grains thoroughly to clear any unwanted substance. Pour both the ingredients plus the mildly washed orange peel into the pot.
3. Set the water to boil at high. When boiling, turn the fire to medium and cook for 45 minutes (or until you see a small tear on the skin). Add in more boiling water if required. Note: Some beans, especially those older or frozen ones might need a little more cooking time. Just watch out for the tear on the skin if so.
4. Pour in the washed lotus seed and boil for another 15 minutes. Add in more boiling water if required.
5. Pour in the lily bulbs and boil for another 30 minutes.
6. Fill up the pot with more boiling water (⁴/₅ pot) and add in the bundled pandan leaves.
7. Slowly stir in the sugar and let it boil for another 10-15 minutes.
8. Scoop to serve either hot or chilled.

"An idealist is one who, on noticing that roses smell better than a cabbage, concludes that it will also make better soup."
H. L. Mencken

PAN ROASTED PHEASANT BREAST WITH SPICED APPLE COMPOTE

Signature Tastes of VANCOUVER

A Vancouver bistro – serving an updated take on traditional French bistro fare prepared by Executive Chef Marc-André Choquette and his talented team. Discover a beautifully renovated interior that combines old world classic bistro elements with modern touches and a French-inspired menu that blends classic culinary flavours of Paris with the use of fresh West Coast ingredients. A dynamic bar scene serves seasonal in-house and classic cocktails and a great selection of local and draft beers on tap as well as an eclectic mix of approachable wines built from the regions of France.

Ingredients:
Pheasant:
4 breast of pheasant
2 tbsp. olive oil
salt, pepper, to taste
4 tbsp. butter
2 sprigs fresh thyme
1 sprig rosemary
1 clove garlic

Spiced Apple Compote:
2 apple
2 tbsp. butter
1 tbsp. honey
¼ tsp. cinnamon
1-2 pc. star anise
¼ tsp. allspice
1 tbsp. calvados, brandy or apple juice

Instructions:
Pheasant:
1. Heat a suitable pan on med-high heat.
2. Season the pheasant with salt and a good crack of pepper. Add the olive oil to the pan. Your oil / pan should be nice and hot.
3. Sear the meat skin side down into the pan, make sure you don't overcrowd the pan.
4. Let the pheasant continue to cook until you have a nice brown colour on the skin.
5. Turn the meat over and turn the heat down. Add the butter, the herbs and the garlic clove to the pan.
6. Let the butter gently foam and brown over the pheasant.
7. Cooking time is approx. 8-10 min depending on the size of the pheasant breasts.

Spiced Apple Compote:
1. Any apple, granny smith, gala or ambrosia will work just fine. Peel, core and dice your apples, about a half inch dice.
2. Heat a small pot on high-med heat. Add your butter. When it starts to melt and foam add your apples.
3. Sauté for a minute or two and then add the honey and the spices.
4. Turn down the heat and cook for another couple minutes. Keep stirring.
5. Add the calvados, brandy, juice and continue to simmer.
6. Serve warm. This compote can be used right away or reserved for later.

TABLEAU BAR BISTRO
1181 MELVILLE STREET, VANCOUVER, BC

"A girl came up to me in a bar and said she wanted to be my apple pie. I wish I'd said something cool, but I was stunned."
Jason Biggs

Located in the Mall complex on Cambie Road , Richmond is the Tandoori Kona Restaurant. This is one of the few Indian restaurants in Richmond. The food served is Northern Indian cuisine which serves mild curries. The Tandoori Kona is a pleasant place that provides good service and is well located with lots of car parking as well. Yes , Tandoori Kona would be a nice place to enjoy some mild Northern Indian cuisine.

Ingredients:
8 C. whole milk, (divided)
2 tbsp. lemon juice
5 C. water, (in a pressure cooker)
1 C. sugar
pinch of saffron
¼ tsp. cardamom powder
2 tbsp. pistachios & almonds, roughly chopped
sugar for the ras, to taste

Instructions:
1. Boil 4 cups milk in a steel pan and boil the remaining 4 cups milk in a non-stick pan (The milk in the non-stick pan needs to be reduced to half the quantity so once it comes to a boil, keep the flame low and keep cooking while stirring occasionally. Grind saffron with a small amount of sugar and add it to the milk while boiling).
2. Once the milk in the steel pan comes to a rolling boil, slowly add lemon juice.
3. When the milk curdles (paneer), switch off the stove and strain the paneer in a cheese cloth.
4. Pour a little cold water over the paneer and hang the cheese cloth on the tap for approx 30 minutes to remove all of the liquid.
5. Remove the paneer from the cheese cloth and run it through a food processor to smooth it out. You can knead the paneer by hand but it will take a long time to make it smooth.
6. Divide the paneer into 12 equal portions a little smaller than the size of a ping pong ball.
7. Roll the portions in your hands until a smooth ball is formed. Lightly press the ball until it flattens out.
8. In the pressure cooker with water, dissolve 1 cup sugar and add the flattened paneer.
9. Close pressure cooker lid and cook until one whistle sounds. Immediately switch off the stove and set the timer for exactly 5 minutes.
10. After 5 minutes, carefully take the pressure cooker to the sink and pour cold water over the lid to remove the pressure.
11. Remove the cooked paneer with a slotted spoon into a bowl and allow it to cool.
12. Meanwhile, the milk in the non-stick pan should have reduced to half. Add sugar to taste, cardamom powder and nuts. Switch off the stove and keep milk aside.
13. Once the paneer is cool enough to handle with your hands, gently squeeze out the sugar syrup from the paneer and place the paneer into a serving dish.
14. Pour the prepared reduced milk over the paneer and chill in the refrigerator.
15. Garnish with additional chopped nuts.

TANDOORI KONA RESTAURANT

11700 CAMBIE ROAD, RICHMOND, BC

"The disparity between a restaurant's price and food quality rises in direct proportion to the size of the pepper mill."
Bryan Miller

Signature Tastes of VANCOUVER

In January 2003, Vince Morlet opened Tapenade Bistro with the idea of bringing an urban bistro to the historic fishing village of Steveston, BC. Over the past several years, Tapenade has earned the reputation of being an exceptional neighbourhood bistro with great food, outstanding service and fantastic wine. The menu is steeped in French tradition, though is updated with West Coast sensibility and is presented in an approachable and informal setting. Our "simple, yet elegant" cuisine showcases the natural beauty of local, sustainable and seasonal ingredients in an appropriate and sumptuous manner.

Ingredients:
1 tbsp. butter
½ C. breadcrumbs
¼ C. parmesan cheese, grated
2½ C. basil, fresh
½ C. parsley
¼ C. olive oil
½ tsp. salt
1 clove garlic
1 lb. ricotta cheese, room temperature
2 lbs. cream cheese, room temperature
½ lb. parmesan cheese, grated
5 eggs
½ C. pine nuts, lightly toasted

Instructions:
1. Preheat oven to 325F degrees.
2. Butter bottom and sides of 10" spring form pan.
3. Mix bread crumbs and ¼ cup Parmesan cheese.
4. Sprinkle mixture into pan, turning to coat completely.
5. Mix basil leaves, parsley, oil, salt and garlic in food processor until smooth paste forms, about 2 minutes, scraping sides occasionally.
6. Put ricotta cheese, cream cheese and Parmesan in a mixer bowl and mix until smooth about 2 minutes.
7. Mix in the eggs.
8. Remove about ⅓ of this mixture to a small bowl.
9. Into the original ⅔ cheese mixture, fold in the basil mixture until well blended.
10. Pour the basil mixture into the prepared pan and carefully spread an even layer of the cheese mixture on top.
11. Sprinkle with pine nuts.
12. Set pan on a baking sheet.
13. Bake 1½ hours.
14. Turn oven off and cool cheesecake about 1 hour with the oven door slightly ajar.
15. Transfer to a rack and cool completely.
16. Serve at room temperature, or slightly warmed.

TAPENADE BISTRO
3711 BAYVIEW STREET, RICHMOND, BC

"All happiness depends on a leisurely breakfast."
John Gunther

MAPLE GLAZED PACIFIC SALMON

Signature Taste of VANCOUVER

Ingredients:
150g fresh salmon (sockeye, spring)
100g Yukon gold nuggets
50g green beans
1 red pepper roasted
25g sherry vinaigrette
25g maple syrup
splash of bourbon
pinch of cinnamon

Instructions:
1. Cook the nuggets until soft. Blanch the beans. Dice the potatoes into ½ inch segments.

2. Cut beans and peppers the same. Pan sear your salmon. Cook to temp required (medium).

3. Mix maple ,cinnamon and bourbon together and coat salmon with it for the last remaining few minutes.

4. Warm up the nuggets, beans, and peppers together, season with salt and fresh cracked pepper.

5. Pour on vinaigrette, toss through the vegetables. Place in middle of the plate, put salmon on top and garnish.

THE ACADEMIC PUBLIC HOUSE
1619 WEST BROADWAY, VANCOUVER, BC

"For all of us who have been involved in the recovery efforts to bring back and strengthen wild salmon runs, we fear that this change in policy could lead to further declines in these wild stocks."
Norm Dicks

Beef Carpaccio and Arugula Salad

Signature Tastes of VANCOUVER

Ingredients:
75 g of AAA Alberta beef tenderloin
50 g Baby Arugula
truffle aioli (garlic mayo with truffle oil)
sea salt
2 crostini
15g of french vinaigrette
shaved fresh parmesan

Instructions:
1. Place thinly sliced beef around plate, sprinkle with salt, dress the Arugula with the French vinaigrette, place in middle of plate.

2. Use a spoon to drizzle truffle aioli around the plate, place the crostini on top of salad, put shaved parmesan on the crostini.

Tip: Cut the beef along grain wrap in saran wrap in to a cylinder shape and freezer over night or a few hours, this will make it easier to cut into thin slices.

THE CALLING PUBLIC HOUSE
1780 DAVIE ST. VANCOUVER, BC

"We don't need a melting pot in this country, folks. We need a salad bowl. In a salad bowl, you put in the different things. You want the vegetables - the lettuce, the cucumbers, the onions, the green peppers - to maintain their identity. You appreciate differences."
Jane Elliot

VEAL PICCATA

I know what you're thinking. The Flying Pig? You must have lots of pork on the menu, right? Nothing could be further from the truth. To be honest, our menu breakdown has a wide range of items and, yes, a small portion can be pork. The Flying Pig represents our desire for you to see the impossible happen every time you visit us.

Ingredients:
½ C. all purpose flour
2 tsp. salt
½ tsp. freshly ground black pepper
4 veal scallops, about ¾ lb. pounded to a thickness of ⅛-inch
1½ tbsp. vegetable oil
5 tbsp. butter
1 C. dry white wine
½ C. chicken stock
1 garlic clove, chopped
1 lemon, juiced, or more to taste, (about 2 tbsp.)
2 tbsp. capers, drained
1 tbsp. chopped parsley leaves, optional, plus sprigs for garnish

Instructions:
1. In a shallow bowl or plate combine the flour, 1½ teaspoons of the salt and pepper and stir to combine thoroughly. Quickly dredge the veal scallops in the seasoned flour mixture, shaking to remove any excess flour.
2. Heat the oil in a large skillet over medium-high heat until very hot but not smoking.
3. Add 1½ tablespoons of the butter and, working quickly and in batches if necessary, cook the veal until golden brown on both sides, about 1 minute per side. Transfer to a plate and set aside.
4. Deglaze the pan with wine and bring to a boil, scraping to remove any browned bits from the bottom of the pan.
5. When the wine has reduced by half, add the chicken stock, chopped garlic, lemon juice and capers and cook for 5 minutes, or until the sauce has thickened slightly.
6. Whisk in the remaining ½ teaspoon of salt, remaining 3½ tablespoons of butter and the chopped parsley.
7. When the butter has melted, return the veal scallops to the pan and cook until heated through and the sauce has thickened, about 1 minute. Garnish with parsley sprigs and serve immediately.

1168 Hamilton Street, Vancouver, BC

THE FLYING PIG

"The only think I like better than talking about Food is eating."
John Walters

CHILI CON CARNE | CUMIN & CHIVE SOUR CREAM | AGED CHEDDAR & LIME

Signature Taste of VANCOUVER

THE MAIN
4210 MAIN STREET, VANCOUVER, BC

Ingredients:
Chili Con Carne:
2 tbsp. good olive oil
2.5 lbs. freshly ground lean Angus beef
1.5 lb. freshly ground Berkshire pork
1 tbsp. good olive oil
2 medium Walla-Walla onions, diced
1 red bell pepper, pith and seeds removed, diced
1 medium Jalapeño pepper, pith and seeds removed, and finely chopped
1 clove organic garlic, minced
20 ml cumin powder
20 ml Mexican oregano
1 tbsp unsweetened cocoa powder
1 tbsp. brown sugar
1 tbsp. chile powder
1 tsp. onion powder
1 tsp. roasted garlic powder
1 tsp. smoked paprika
1 tsp. Ancho chile powder
1 tsp. Cascabel chile powder
1 pinch cayenne pepper
1 dried bay leaf
½ chipotle pepper blended with 2 tbsp. adobo sauce
20 ml balsamic reduction
1 bottle of dark beer
2 oz. bourbon
2 C. homemade chicken stock (or quality organic store bought)
3 C. strained tomato sauce
2 C. canned, diced tomatoes
1 tbsp. BBQ sauce*
1 tsp. Worcestershire sauce
1 tsp. srirachia hot sauce
2 C. fresh corn kernels
5 roma tomatoes, roughly diced
2 x 14 oz can – pinto beans, drained & gently rinsed*
coarse salt and freshly cracked black pepper to taste
*OPTIONAL
Cumin & Chive Sour Cream + Additional Garnishes:
250 ml full fat organic sour cream (drained in cheese cloth over night)
1 tbsp. toasted cumin
2 tbsp. finely chopped chives
juice of ½ a lime
grated aged white cheddar as needed
cilantro sprigs as needed
fresh lime wedges as needed

Instructions:
Chili Con Carne:
1. In a large ovenproof ceramic coated, or cast iron pot, brown beef & pork in olive oil, over medium high heat until well caramelized and crispy in places. Next, season the mixture generously with coarse salt and freshly ground black pepper. Remove from pot and reserve. Place pot back onto heat.
2. Add additional olive oil, onion, bell pepper, jalapeño pepper and garlic to pot. Cook until onions begin to caramelize, approximately 5 – 8 minutes.
3. Next, add cumin, oregano, cocoa powder, brown sugar, chile powder, onion powder, garlic powder, smoked paprika, Ancho chile powder, Cascabel chile powder and cayenne pepper. Cook for 2 – 3 minutes to toast spices.
4. Add chipotle pepper with adobo sauce, balsamic reduction, beer, bourbon, chicken stock, tomato sauce, canned diced tomatoes, BBQ sauce, Worcestershire sauce and sriracha sauce. Season to taste with coarse salt and freshly cracked black pepper and bring to a simmer.
5. Cover and place chilli into a pre-heated, 350 degree oven and bake for 1 hour, stirring occasionally.
6. Remove lid from pot, add corn, tomatoes and pinto beans. Return chilli to oven, turn down to 300 degrees and continue to cook uncovered for 1.5 hours.
7. Remove and allow the chilli to cool for 40 minutes. Top with a dollop of cumin & chive sour cream and a pinch of aged white cheddar. Serve with a slice of lime and a few sprigs of cilantro.

Cumin & Chive Sour Cream:
1. Combine all ingredients in a small bowl. Chill until ready to serve.

"Grey cloth coaxes the lime trees of friends shadowing berries dropped by the grateful earth."
Bradley Chicho

CORNED BEEF HASH

The Oakwood Canadian Bistro, a casual neighbourhood room specializing in down-to-earth Canadian fare. The Oakwood Canadian Bistro's food philosophy is focused on fresh, house-made dishes crafted from locally sourced products. The seasonally changing menu caters to market availability and the sustainability of the products. All meats are organic, local and free of hormones and antibiotics, while the seafood is sustainable, seasonal and Ocean Wise certified. From the breads and pastas to the butchery and sauces, all products are made in-house with quality and consistency. The Oakwood Canadian Bistro serves fresh, honest food in a casual neighbourhood environment.

Ingredients:
2-3 tbsp. unsalted butter
1 medium onion, finely chopped (about 1 C.)
2-3 C. finely chopped, cooked corned beef
2-3 C. chopped cooked potatoes, preferably Yukon gold
salt and pepper
chopped fresh parsley

Instructions:
1. Heat butter in a large skillet (preferably cast iron) on medium heat. Add the onion and cook a few minutes, until translucent.
2. Mix in the chopped corned beef and potatoes. Spread out evenly over the pan. Increase the heat to high or medium high and press down on the mixture with a metal spatula.
3. Do not stir the potatoes and corned beef, but let them brown. If you hear them sizzling, this is good. Use a metal spatula to peak underneath and see if they are browning. If nicely browned, use the spatula to flip sections over in the pan so that they brown on the other side. Press down again with the spatula. If there is too much sticking, you can add a little more butter to the pan. Continue to cook in this manner until the potatoes and the corned beef are nicely browned.
4. Remove from heat, stir in chopped parsley. Add plenty of freshly ground black pepper, and add salt to taste.
5. Serve with fried or poached eggs for breakfast.

THE OAKWOOD CANADIAN BISTRO
2741 WEST 4TH AVENUE, VANCOUVER, BC

"An Irish beer cannot be complete without a plate of corned beef and cabbage. One cannot be savored fully without the other."
Sergio Valadez

GROUSE MOUNTAIN RESORTS LTD.
6400 Nancy Greene Way, North Vancouver
British Columbia, Canada V7R 4K9
Reservations 604.980.9311
Fax 604.984.7534
grousemountain.com

Open 5pm – 10pm daily

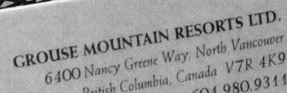

THE OBSERVATORY
AT GROUSE MOUNTAIN

Proud members of both the Green Table Network and Ocean Wise

Chua

SEARED QUALLICUM BAY SCALLOPS

Welcome to The Observatory, Grouse Mountain's finest restaurant - taking standards of food, beverage, and hospitality to new heights. The Observatory's contemporary BC menu harnesses the remarkable confluence of local flavours and worldly techniques that give the province its unique character. Chef Dino L. Gazzola is dedicated to sourcing the finest and freshest regional ingredients available, creating memorable dining experiences for the discerning palate.

Ingredients:
6 mid sized fresh quallicum bay scallops
½ C. forbidden rice
10 shiso leaves
2 pcs. fresh sea urchin roe
2 C. fish stock
2 tsp. white soy sauce
2 tbsp. grapeseed oil
4 tsp. cold unsalted butter

Instructions:
1. Combine forbidden rice and fish stock in heavy bottomed pot. Cover and bring to a boil over medium heat. Reduce heat and simmer 20 minutes.
2. Add 2 tsp of butter and stir to combine.
3. Bring 1 litre of water to a rolling boil.
4. Add shiso leaves and cook 20 seconds.
5. Remove from water and quickly plunge into ice water to cool.
6. Remove shiso from ice water and gently squeeze to remove excess water. Puree in blender with enough cold water to make a smooth sauce. Strain through a fine sieve and adjust seasoning.
7. Remove abductor muscle from scallops (located on side of scallop). Pat scallops dry with a clean towel to remove excess moisture.
8. Heat grapeseed oil, in a non stick pan, over high heat until oil shimmers.
9. Carefully place scallops in oil and cook for 30 seconds. Turn and cook an additional.
10. Remove from heat and add 2 tsp butter, spooning over scallops when melted.
11. Dived forbidden rice equally onto two plates.
12. Garnish with sea urchin and white soy.
13. Top with scallops and shiso puree.

"The worst vice of the solitary is the worship of his food."
Cyril Connolly

Spinach and Cheddar Omelette

Red Wagon is a diner, full stop. Unlike other revisionist salutes to lunch counters past, the room is not all fancied up, thank God. It has retained the wobbly tables, giant plate-glass windows that showcase snowcapped mountains over a foreground of dirty streetscape, and groovy retro light fixtures of the many lowbrow cafés that inhabited the space before.

Signature Tastes of VANCOUVER

Ingredients:
12 large eggs
½ C. sour cream
1 tsp. salt
¾ tsp. freshly ground pepper
¼ tsp. baking powder
1 (10-oz.) package frozen, thawed, and well-drained chopped spinach
2 tbsp. butter or margarine
6 small plum tomatoes, seeded and chopped
2 C. (8 oz.) shredded cheddar cheese
½ C. cooked, crumbled bacon

Instructions:
1. Beat first 6 ingredients at medium-high speed with an electric mixer 2 to 3 minutes or until well blended.

2. Melt butter in a 12-inch ovenproof skillet; add egg mixture.

3. Bake at 350º for 15 minutes. Remove from oven; sprinkle with tomatoes, cheese, and bacon. Return to oven, and bake 15 to 20 more minutes or until set. Serve immediately.

2296 East Hastings Street, Vancouver, BC

The Red Wagon

"Just as there is nothing between the admirable omelet and the intolerable, so with autobiography."
Hilaire Belloc

HOMEMADE CLAM CHOWDER

The Sandbar Seafood Restaurant is a 300-seat restaurant in the heart of Granville Island. With its very own sushi bar, Sandbar has earned bragging rights as a fresh seafood restaurant. Their unique, second-floor patio is perched right beneath the Granville Street Bridge, overlooking False Creek. This covered patio is the perfect spot to soak in the sun and enjoy some of Vancouver's freshest seafood. This is one of many reasons why Sandbar has won "Best Restaurant to take Out-of-Town Guests" 2 years in a row.

Ingredients:
2 tbsp. butter
2 slices thick cut bacon, chopped
1 medium onion, chopped
2 stalks celery & leaves, chopped
2 carrots, chopped into small pieces
4 sprigs fresh thyme
salt and pepper
2 tsp. hot sauce, eyeball it
2 tbsp. all-purpose flour
1 pint half-and-half
3 C. chicken stock, from soup aisle
1 C. raw hash brown potatoes, from dairy aisle of the market
2 (10 oz.) cans baby clams, and their juice

Instructions:
1. In a medium pot over medium high heat melt butter. Add bacon, onions, celery, carrot, and thyme sprigs. Season with salt, pepper and hot sauce and cook 5 minutes. Add flour and cook a minute more.

2. Add half-and-half and stock and bring to a bubble, then stir in potatoes and clams. Bring soup back to a boil, reduce heat and simmer 15 minutes, until potatoes are cooked and soup has thickened to coat the back of a spoon.

3. Remove the thyme sprigs from the soup. The thyme leaves will have fallen off into the soup. Stir and adjust seasonings in your soup. Pour soup into mugs. Top with shredded cheese or green onions if desired.

THE SANDBAR SEAFOOD
1535 JOHNSTON STREET, VANCOUVER, BC

"Men are Clams, Women are Crowbars."
David Clarke

THE TEAHOUSE FAMOUS STUFFED MUSHROOMS

Nestled in the heart of Stanley Park sits Teahouse Restaurant; serving some of Vancouver's best cuisine since 1978. The panoramic ocean views at this romantic spot located at Ferguson Point earned Teahouse the title of 'Best Sunset in the City'. Along with the scenery, Teahouse offers the warmth and charm of a historic house, and delicious, West Coast cuisine using fresh, local ingredients. This iconic restaurant has a casual yet sophisticated atmosphere that comes alive at night. Beautifully lit, there is a fireplace in every room, adding a delightful glow to the evening mood and taking the chill off any rainy Vancouver night. A scenic drive into Stanley Park brings you to Ferguson Point, so stop in for a bite, enjoy a glass of wine and indulge in the longest sunset in the city.

Ingredients:
24 white mushrooms
8 oz. firm cream cheese
2 tbsp. sour cream
1-2 chopped green onions
1 clove minced garlic
2 oz. grated Emmenthal cheese
2 oz. crab meat
2 oz. shrimp meat
2 oz. melted butter
salt and pepper to taste

Instructions:
1. Pre-heat oven to 375 degrees.

2. Remove stems from 24 clean mushroom caps.

3. Place caps on lightly greased cookie sheet.

4. Brush inside of caps with butter.

5. Mix remaining ingredients together (saving ½ of the Emmenthal for topping).

6. Fill mushroom caps with mixture.

7. Bake for 10 minutes.

8. Top with remaining Emmenthal and broil till brown.

9. Serve immediately.

Signature Tastes of VANCOUVER

THE TEAHOUSE IN STANLEY PARK
7501 STANLEY PARK DRIVE, VANCOUVER, BC

"If more of us valued food and cheer above hoarded gold, it would be a much merrier world."
J.R.R. Tolkien

TIM HORTON'S CHILI

The Tim Horton's chain was founded in 1964 in Hamilton, Ontario. The chain's focus on top quality, always fresh product, value, great service and community leadership has allowed it to grow into the largest quick service restaurant chain in Canada specializing in always fresh coffee, baked goods and homestyle lunches. Tim Horton's locations can presently be found in Michigan, Maine, Connecticut, Ohio, West Virginia, Kentucky, Pennsylvania, Rhode Island, Massachusetts and New York, with responsible expansion continuing in these core markets. The Canadian operation is 95% franchise owned and operated, and plans in the U.S. call for the same key strategy to be implemented as expansion progresses. Currently, there are more than 3,000 restaurants across Canada, and over 600 locations in the United States.

Ingredients:
2 lbs. ground beef
1 tbsp. olive oil
2 12 onions (diced)
3 celery ribs (diced)
1 green pepper (diced)
19 oz. kidney beans
(dark red kidney beans
rinsed drained)
20 oz. mushroom (pieces
drained chopped)
20 oz. tomato soup
(undiluted)
28 oz. diced tomatoes
(with juice)
2 tbsp. chili powder
(divided)
1 tsp. oregano
1 tsp. salt
¼ tsp. pepper
1 tsp. sugar
1½ garlic cloves (minced
or 3 tsp. garlic powder)

Instructions:
1. Brown the ground beef in the olive oil in a large frying pan over medium heat until no longer pink; place in a large pot. Do not drain.
2. Sauté onion, celery and green pepper in the drippings, in the same frying pan used for the ground beef, for about 5 minutes until onion is translucent.
3. Add a little of the chili powder.
4. Add sautéed veggies to the ground beef.
5. Add rinsed and drained kidney beans, mushrooms pieces, undiluted tomato soup and tomatoes with the liquid.
6. Add the rest of the chili powder, oregano, salt, pepper, sugar, and garlic.
7. Stir ingredients together well.
8. Cover and simmer for one hour, stirring occasionally.
9. Remove cover and simmer for 30 minutes or more, stirring occasionally.

1752 DAVIE STREET, VANCOUVER, BC

TIM HORTON'S

"Three things are needed for a good life, good friends, good food, and good song."
Jason Zebehazy

MARINATED SABLEFISH

If one ever needed a reason to go to Vancouver, eating at Tojo's new restaurant at 1133 West Broadway is reason enough. Tojo, you see, is not just a master sushi chef, he's the veritable Picasso of sushi chefs. He can bend a slice of raw fish over a rectangle of rice in a way more satisfying than David Beckham can bend a soccer ball towards the goal on a free kick. He can colour your palate with delicacies that make you want to sing a high C like Pavarotti.

Ingredients:
⅓ C. dark soy sauce
¼ C. mirin or sake or white wine
1 tbsp. granulated sugar
2 tsp. ground ginger
4 skinless sablefish fillets (each 3 oz)
2 tsp. olive oil
1 bunch spinach, washed and tough stems removed, if necessary
1 tsp. grated garlic

Instructions:
1. In a small bowl, combine soy sauce, mirin (or sake or white wine), sugar, and ginger until well mixed.
2. Pour the marinade into a large, clean food-grade plastic bag (or a plastic container, with a lid, that is just large enough to hold the fish).
3. Add sablefish fillets, pushing them into the marinade. Squeeze out as much air as possible and seal the bag tightly with an elastic band, close to the fish (or put the lid on the plastic container).
4. Refrigerate overnight or for up to 2 days.
5. Preheat the oven to 450°f. Lightly grease a baking sheet.
6. Pat dry the sablefish fillets, then place them on the baking sheet. Discard the marinade. Bake the fillets until the fish is cooked through and flakes easily, 10 to 12 minutes.
7. While the fish is cooking, heat the olive oil in a frying pan on high heat. Add spinach and garlic and stir until the greens are wilted.
8. Remove from the heat and season with salt and pepper.
9. To serve, divide the spinach among four warmed plates. Top with a sablefish fillet and serve immediately.

TOJO'S RESTAURANT
1133 WEST BROADWAY, VANCOUVER, BC

"Not eating meat is a decision, eating meat is an instinct."
Denis Leary

CALIFORNIA BURGER

The Topanga Cafe is awesome. I was introduced to it through my husband who has been enjoying dinners there with his family since childhood. The service is so friendly and the food is delicious. Recommendations (especially if you are veggie): the enchilada with eggplant and beans and a Dos Equis. For dessert: their famous chocolate cake. Warm staff and atmosphere and wonderful comfort food.

Signature Tastes of VANCOUVER

Ingredients:
1 lb. ground beef
4 sesame seed buns
1 lb. mushrooms sliced
and grilled
12 slices avocado
4 slices jack cheese
4 slices tomato
4 tsp. thousand island
salad dressing

Instructions:
1. Cook burger to desired doneness.

2. Pan toast rolls with small amount of butter then spread with thousand island dressing.

3. Place grilled burger on roll and garnish.

2904 WEST 4TH AVENUE, VANCOUVER, BC

TOPANGA CAFÉ

"I said to my friends that if I was going to starve, I might as well starve where the food is good."
Virgil Thomson

White Cannellini Bean and Pancetta Soup

Simple and fresh is really what Italian home cooking is all about. At Trattoria the menu reads like a summer in Italy, with classic ingredients, masterfully combined, and served without a lot of fuss and bother. This is what Italian food should be.

Ingredients:
1 C. white cannellini beans (cooked)
100 g Pancetta (roughly chopped)
½ C. white onion (diced)
½ C. celery (diced)
1.5 L chicken stock
2 cloves garlic (crushed)
30 ml olive oil
to taste salt and pepper
1 tbsp. butter (big cube)

Instructions:
1. Sweat off the pancetta, garlic, celery and onion in the olive oil until tender.

2. Add the chicken stock and slowly bring to simmer.

3. Add the white beans and bring to a simmer, cook for 7 minutes.

4. Add the butter and stir until melted, taste and finish with salt and pepper.

TRATTORIA ITALIAN KITCHEN
1850 WEST 4TH AVENUE, VANCOUVER, BC

"I live on good soup, not on fine words."
Moliere

Signature Tastes of VANCOUVER

Freshly in from the hinterlands, the former proprietors of the "Wood Restaurant" in Fernie, BC (voted 'Best Resort Restaurant in North America 2003' and listed in 'Where to eat in Canada') have arrived with their legendary bistro menu and small town friendliness to launch a new adventure under the bright lights of Granville St. The Twisted Fork is classic french dining made simple, all the flavours, all the tender care but with a little less fuss. With a tendency towards cream and butter, fresh homegrown ingredients, rich tasty sauces, baked house breads and featuring some of the mainstays of bistro dining such as confit duck, oxtail soup, mussels with frites and frog legs.

Ingredients:
2 - 3 lb. chicken
4 - 5 lb. Muscovy or King Cole duck
10 - 12 lb. turkey

Stuffing:
1lb. sausage meat (pork)
8 oz. chopped raw chicken livers
4 oz. dry cranberries
8 oz. stale bread (crumbed and soaked in buttermilk)
1 onion and 2 stalks celery chopped and sautéd until tender
1 tsp. dry sage
¼ - ½ C. port
salt and pepper

Instructions:
Method for Boning:
1. Remove wish bone by making two slices on either side of each bone … run thumb and index finger up each side to loosen wish bone …then pull to remove.
2. Stand the bird on its head so the tail bone is up (Parson's nose) … using a strong knife cut straight down the back bone on one side of the tail … repeat on the other side of tail to remove back bone in one piece.
3. To remove legs … scrape flesh down the sides of the bone until you reach the knuckle… chop off knuckle and pull out bone.
4. Cut off wings … you don't need them.
5. To remove rib and breast plate … use tip of knife and follow close to bone to remove carridge.
6. All bones of the duck and chicken are removed as they are inside the turduckin … leave the wings and drumsticks of the turkey on to give the turduckin structure while roasting.
NOTE: You can make this and store it in the fridge, BUT once you stuff the Turduckin you must roast it off…do not stuff the Turduckin and then store in the fridge for health reasons…raw bird and stuffing do not hold so roast it right away!)

Stuffing:
1. Lay the turkey down skin side to the board. Season heavily. Spread a modest layer of stuffing.
2. Place duck skin side down on the turkey. Season and apply more stuffing.
3. Place chicken skin side down on the duck. Season and stuffing.
4. Pull the outsides of turkey to hold contents of the turduckin.
5. Using a butcher's needle and twine sow up the back of the turkey. Tuck the turkey wings under and the drumsticks in front of bird.
6. Place turduckin on a vegetable trivet in a large roasting pan. Roast 1st hour at 375F. Roast and baste 2nd hour at 325F. Roast till done at 275F … internal temperature should read 182F to ensure centre is cooked. 10 lb. turkey in this method will roast for 4 - 5 hours.
7. Serve with your favourite side dishes such as mashed or roasted potatoes, turnip and squash.

TWISTED FORK BISTRO
1147 GRANVILLE STREET, VANCOUVER, BC

"If you are ever at a loss to support a flagging conversation, introduce the subject of eating."
Leigh Hunt

Fish Soup

Enticing cocktails, refined wines, eclectic import beers – Uva Wine Bar, located adjacent to the Moda Hotel, is Downtown Vancouver's enclave for connoisseurs of wines and spirits seeking a sanctuary that caresses the eye as well as the palate.

Ingredients:
1 lb. cod or 1 lb. red snapper or 1 lb. halibut steaks, cut into 1 in. cubes
4 tbsp. butter (olive oil)
1 large onion, chopped
1 green pepper, chopped
3 garlic cloves, minced
fresh oregano
fresh thyme
1 (15 oz.) can stewed tomatoes
3 (15 oz.) cans chicken broth (veg will do)
8 oz. clam juice
4 red potatoes (optional)
sourdough bread (rolls or baguette)
white wine
1 C. mayonnaise
2 garlic cloves (to taste)
lemon juice
cayenne pepper (to taste)

Instructions:
1. This is a very basic recipe, it encourages experimentation with additional ingredients.
2. In large saucepan saute butter, pepper, onion, and garlic until onion is translucent.
3. Add chicken broth, tomatoes and clam juice, and potatoes if necessary, bring to boil; reduce heat to simmer.
4. Add fresh herbs, splash of wine, salt and pepper to taste and let simmer for 3 minutes (or until potatoes are tender) stirring occasionally.
5. Add fish and cook for 5-7 minutes or until fish is cooked.
6. While fish is cooking in soup, make the aioli.
7. In small bowl mix, mayo, garlic, lemon juice and cayenne.
8. Put on the table.
9. Serve soup in large bowls with plenty of sourdough and dollop of aioli.

UVA WINE BAR
900 SEYMOUR STREET, VANCOUVER, BC

Signature Taste of VANCOUVER

"I did my famous cabbage soup diet, so I was able to do it."
Ellen Burstyn

SPICE-ENCRUSTED LAMB POPSICLES

Signature Tastes of VANCOUVER

Vikram Vij and Meeru Dhalwala have been running Vij's since September 1994. Our restaurant has stood out from other Indian Restaurants, because we do not serve what is typically expected. We enjoy combining spices from, say, Gujurat, with spices from Punjab. We avoid using a tandoor oven, since it's already so commonplace elsewhere. Our food philosophy has always been to keep our spices and cooking techniques Indian — from all regions of India — while using meats, seafood and produce that are locally available. To this effect, we change our menu seasonally.

Ingredients:
3½ – 4 lbs. rack of lamb cut into 30 chops
½ C. cooking oil
2 tbsp. ground cumin
1½ tsp. salt
1 to 1½ tsp. ground cayenne pepper
2 tbsp. ground coriander
1 tbsp. paprika
1 tsp. turmeric
2 tbsp. finely chopped garlic
½ – 1 lemon cut in wedges (optional)

Instructions:
1. In a large bowl, combine lamb with oil, spices and garlic. Toss lightly to coat the lamb, then cover and refrigerate for 2 – 3 hours.
2. Move oven rack to highest position and preheat oven to 500°F.
3. On a large baking sheet, arrange chops without overlapping and bake for two minutes.
4. Remove from oven, turn chops over and bake for two more minutes.
5. Cut into a popsicle; it should be pink in the centre. If not, bake each side for 30 seconds to one minute longer.
6. Transfer to serving platter and squeeze lemon juice.
7. If you have time, Vij says, marinate the night before to enhance the flavour.

1480 W 11TH AVE, VANCOUVER, BC

VIJ'S

"One cannot think well, love well, sleep well, if one has not dined well."
Virginia Woolf

Vij's Rangoli uniquely doubles as a market and a restaurant. We sell frozen and refrigerated ready-to-eat Indian dishes, freshly roasted and ground Indian spices, as well as our cookbooks - Vij's: Elegant and Inspired Indian Cuisine and Vij's at Home: Relax, Honey.

Ingredients:
2½ C. (600 ml.) of whole milk
⅓ C. (66 g.) of uncooked short grain white rice
pinch of salt
1 egg
¼ C. (50 g.) dark brown sugar
1 tsp. of vanilla extract
¼ tsp. of cinnamon
⅓ C. (40 g.) raisins

Instructions:

1. In a medium-sized, heavy-bottomed saucepan, bring the milk, rice and salt to a boil over high heat. Reduce heat to low and simmer until the rice is tender, about 20-25 minutes. Stir frequently to prevent the rice from sticking to the bottom of the pan.

2. In a small mixing bowl, whisk together egg and brown sugar until well mixed. Add a half cup of the hot rice mixture to the egg mixture, a tablespoon at a time, vigorously whisking to incorporate.

3. Add egg mixture back into the saucepan of rice and milk and stir, on low heat, for 10 minutes or so, until thickened. Be careful not to have the mixture come to a boil at this point. Stir in the vanilla. Remove from heat and stir in the raisins and cinnamon.

4. Serve warm or cold.

1488 WEST 11 AVENUE, VANCOUVER, BC

VIJ'S RANGOLI

"After a good dinner one can forgive anybody, even one's own relatives."
Oscar Wilde

FOUR O'CLOCK COCKTAIL
SEASON: AUTUMN

Recognized as the 'jewel in Vancouver's culinary crown', West's outstanding contemporary regional cuisine and seamless service has earned much critical acclaim. Pristine seasonal ingredients are sourced to deliver superbly conceived dishes offering modern interpretations of classics.

Signature Taste of VANCOUVER

Ingredients:
Cocktail:
1 oz. Makers Mark Bourbon
1 oz. Grand Marnier Cordon Rouge
1 small sugar cube
½ oz. water
3 dashes Fee Brothers whisky barrel aged bitters (or Agnostura with one clove)
½ oz. fresh lemon juice

Garnish:
Navan (vanilla cognac), orange blossom, lemon foam
5 oz. Navan (vanilla cognac made by Grand Marnier)
5 oz. fresh squeezed orange juice
4 oz. fresh squeezed lemon juice
10 oz. simple syrup
2 tsp. orange blossom water
5½ sheets gelatin

Instructions:
Cocktail:
1. Place small sugar cube in a mixing glass, add 3 dashes of Bitters, and ½ oz water, and dissolve.
2. Add in the 1oz Makers Mark, 1oz Grand Marnier, and ½ oz lemon juice.
3. Add ice to sleeve and stir until well chilled.
4. Strain into a chilled martini glass.
5. Top with the Vanilla citrus foam.

Garnish:
1. Place all of the liquid ingredients into a bowl. 'Bloom' the 5½ sheets of gelatin in cold water to soften.
2. Warm 4oz of the juices etc. and dissolve the bloomed gelatin into the mixture.
3. Place in the refrigerator for a couple of hours until it becomes 'loosely' gelatinous.
4. Spoon the gelatin mixture into a whipped cream dispenser and charge with two charges of nitrous oxide.
5. Chill the dispenser for one more hour, shake well and dispense.
Note: The foam should keep its consistency as long as the drink is very cold, and once either the drink warms up or the surrounding air warms the foam it should 'fall' into a liquid form, adding another dimension to the cocktail. On a warm day use another half sheet of gelatin for a stiffer consistency.

Taste Profile: A slightly sweet yet tart candy like entrance through the vanilla orange blossom foam leading to a savory bourbon experience with a touch of clove and cinnamon with a hint of bitter spiciness on the finish.

WEST RESTAURANT

2881 GRANVILLE STREET, VANCOUVER, BC

"An alcoholic is someone you don't like who drinks as much as you do."
Dylan Thomas

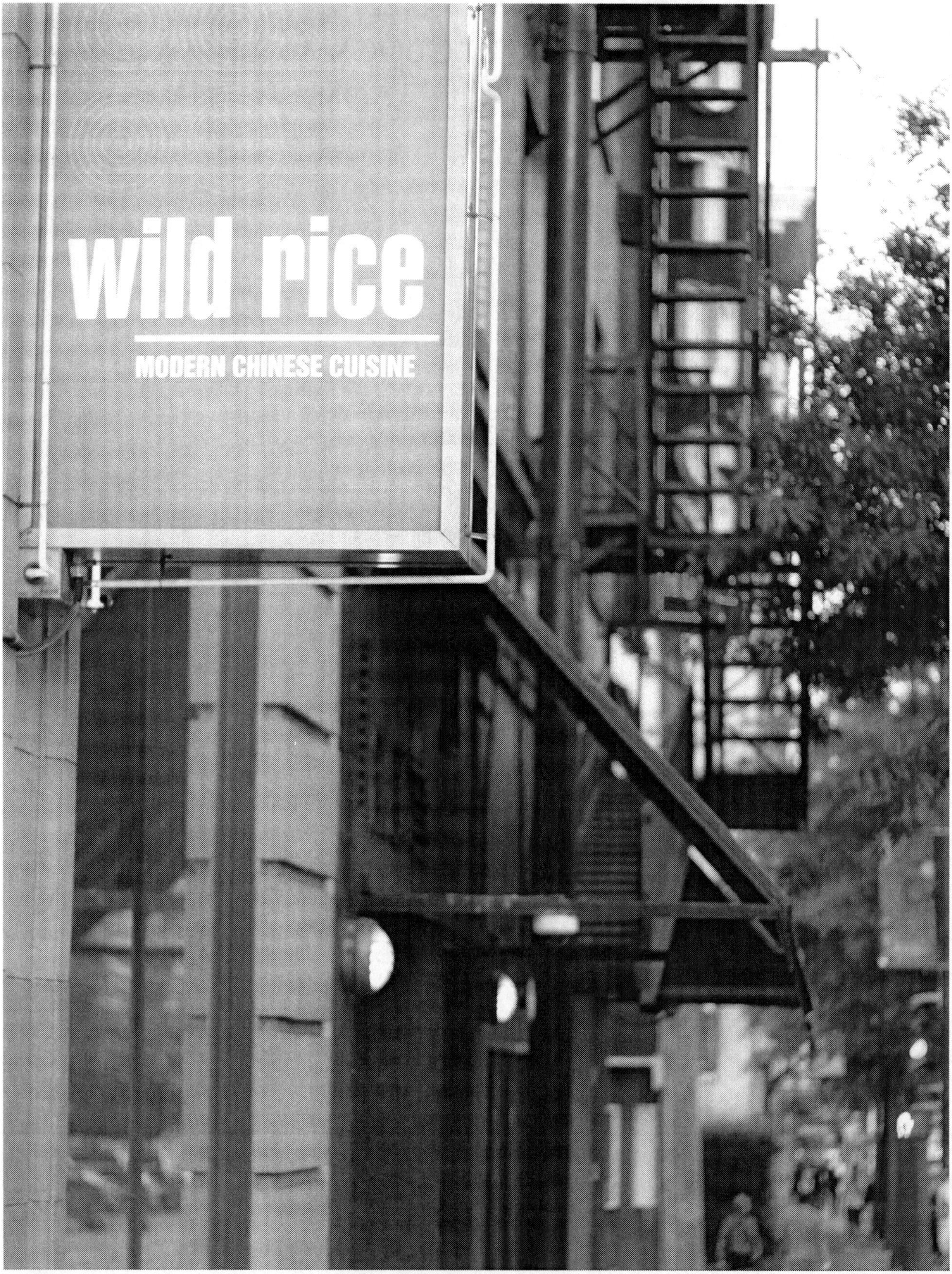
wild rice
MODERN CHINESE CUISINE

SPOT PRAWN HA GOW

The restaurant and hospitality industry is an integral part of Andrew's heritage. Andrew got an early start on his restaurant career starting at the tender age of 13. Upon graduation Andrew and a friend opened his first restaurant venture – The Brickhouse on Main Street. For years Andrew had dreamed of creating a modern chinese bistro. The sale of his share in The Brickhouse allowed him to pursue that dream and Wild Rice was born in 2001 – ironically, next door to The Lotus Hotel founded by his grandfather. Always a believer in using local ingredients to create Wild Rice's unique cuisine, Andrew has gone on to strengthen his commitment to supporting local and sustainable food.

Ingredients:
1 lb. (454 g) B.C. spot prawns
1 tsp. (5 mL) fresh ginger, grated on micro-plane
¼ C. (60 mL) green onions, finely diced
¼ C. (60 mL) water chestnuts, minced
1 tbsp. (15 mL) sesame oil
2 tbsp. (30 mL) oyster sauce
freshly ground pepper
8 oz. (225 g) hagou flour
½ C. (125 mL) red vinegar
½ C. (125 mL) mirin
1 tbsp. (15 mL) cilantro, chiffonaded

Instructions:
1. Peel prawns and, using a small knife, split each prawn in half lengthwise along the back and remove the intestinal tract.
2. Using a cleaver, dice the prawns into large chunks, then smear them on the chopping board with the side of the cleaver. Chop finely. If you don't have a cleaver, mince them very fine.
3. Place minced prawns in a mixing bowl and add ginger, green onions, water chestnuts, sesame oil, oyster sauce and pepper and green onions until the ingredients bind together.
4. Make up the hagou flour into a dough as per the directions on the packet.
5. Make sure your working space is well oiled and knead the dough until it becomes shiny and not sticky.
6. Separate the dough into half-ounce (15 g) chunks and roll out each dough chunk very thinly, until it almost becomes translucent.
7. Cut out a round of the dough using a 10cm pastry cutter to make each hagou wrapper.
8. Place a large spoonful of the prawn mixture into the centre of the wrapper.
9. Fold one side over to touch the other, roll onto its back and crimp the edges together to seal.
10. Steam for 6 minutes in a bamboo steamer basket.
11. Combine the red vinegar, mirin and cilantro in a small bowl and whisk together. Serve on the side with the hagou.

117 WEST PENDER STREET, VANCOUVER, BC

WILD RICE

"I am not a glutton - I am an explorer of food"
Erma Bombeck

YEW
restaurant + bar

ROYAL GALA APPLE BC BLUEBERRY PIE

Signature Tastes of VANCOUVER

Ingredients:
Pie Dough:
3 C. bread flour
1½ C. cake flour
⅛ tsp. salt
16 oz. butter, cold and diced
1 C. ice cold water
¼ C. ice cold cream

Pie Filling:
4 C. of peeled cored and diced fresh Royal Gala apples
1½ C. fresh or frozen BC grown blueberries
1 vanilla bean, cut in half lengthwise
¾ C. apple juice
1 C. sugar
3 tbsp. corn starch
4 tbsp. butter

Instructions:
Pie Dough:
1. In a Kitchen Aid mixer, using the paddle attachment, mix at low speed both flours and salt for about 30 seconds.
2. Add the diced cold butter and continue mixing until the butter almost disappears. Pour in both cold water and cream, and mix until the dough comes together. Empty the dough on a floured working surface and continue mixing until properly mixed.
3. Wrap into food grade plastic wrap and refrigerate for at least 4 hours.

Pie Filling:
1. In a large heavy duty pot, place the diced apple, vanilla bean and apple juice and bring to a low simmer.
2. Add the corn starch to the sugar and stir together then add the mix to the simmering apples. Gently stir until completely incorporated and cook for about 15 minutes over low heat.
3. Pour the mixture into a deep tray and let cool at room temperature. Once cool, fold in the blueberries.

Pie Making:
1. Pre heat the oven at 350F.
2. Using a wooden rolling pin, roll the pie dough on a well floured surface down to about ⅓ centimeter thick. Roll enough dough that besides covering the inside of a 8 inch deep dish pie it also overlaps the sides by about 2 centimeters.
3. Fill the pie with the cold pie filling, adding extra filling (a well rounded mountain effect to the pie). Roll extra dough to create the top of the pie and place over the bottom part.
4. Using a fork, press gently around the edge to seal the pie and with a knife cut off the excess dough.
5. In the middle top of the pie, create a chimney opening to let the steam escape during baking. Using a baking brush, apply some cream to the top of the pie and sprinkle the top with some sugar.
6. Place in the oven and bake for about 30 to 40 minutes until the top of the pie is a nice golden color. Baking time will depend on the type and size of your oven, so please adjust accordingly.

"There is one thing more exasperating than a wife who can cook and won't, and that's a wife who can't cook and will."
Robert Frost

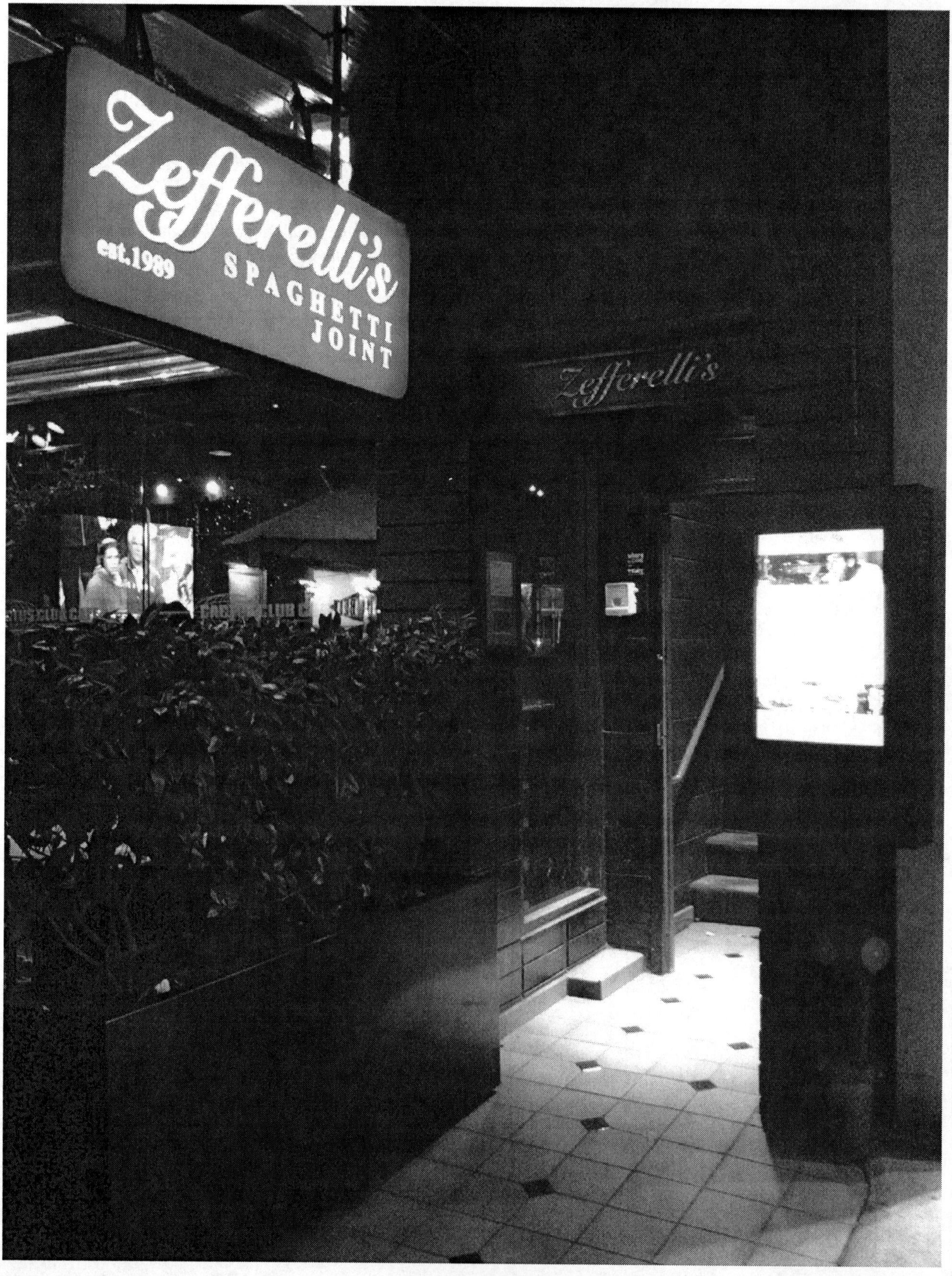
Zefferelli's
est.1989
SPAGHETTI
JOINT
Zefferelli's

Zefferelli's is a sophisticated, warm spot upstairs on Robson Street featuring a menu of rustic, authentic Italian cuisine. The menu is standard Italian fare, no surprises there. This place is not for the daring. Reliably good pasta, if a tad boring. The portions are quite large too.

Ingredients:
100 ml. olive oil
1 medium-hot red chilli, deseeded and finely chopped
1 fat garlic clove, finely chopped
3 pared strips of lemon zest, finely chopped
450 g. linguine
2 tbsp. lemon juice, plus lemon wedges to serve
225g freshly cooked white crab meat
2 tbsp. chopped fresh flatleaf parsley

Instructions:
1. Put the olive oil, chilli, garlic and lemon zest into a small pan and put over a gentle heat until it begins to sizzle. Remove from the heat and set aside.

2. Bring a large saucepan of well-salted water to the boil. Add the linguine and cook for 8-9 minutes, or until al dente. Drain well and set aside.

3. Tip the chilli and lemon mixture into the pan the pasta was in, then add the lemon juice and season. Heat until sizzling, then add the linguine and crab meat to the pan and toss gently over a medium heat to warm the crab through.

4. Add the parsley, season, and serve immediately with lemon wedges.

1136 ROBSON STREET, VANCOUVER, BC

ZEFFERELLI'S

"The only real stumbling block is fear of failure. In cooking you've got to have a what-the-hell attitude."
Julia Child

zipang sushi

tel: 604-708-16

GOMAAE

The restaurant itself is cute, a combination of tables and booths, and large framed poster art (maybe magazine covers) hanging on the walls. It's super casual, you can just pop in should you be in the sushi mood. Service was good, cute staff, and they were pretty attentive.

Ingredients:
1 lb. fresh spinach, washed
4 tbsp. roasted black sesame seeds
2 tbsp. sake, boiled and cooled
2 tbsp. sugar
1½ tbsp. soy sauce

Instructions:
1. Boil lots of water in a large pot. Boil spinach in the boiling water for about one minute. Drain and soak the spinach in water until cool.
2. Drain and squeeze the spinach to remove the excess liquid.
3. Cut spinach into about 2-inch lengths and set aside.
4. Put sesame seeds in a suribachi mortar and grind well with a surikogi pestle. Or, place sesame seeds in a blender or food processor and grind until smooth.
5. Add sugar and mix well.
6. Further, add soy sauce and sake and mix until combined.
7. Season boiled spinach with the sesame sauce.

ZIPANG SUSHI
3710 MAIN STREET, VANCOUVER, BC

"You can't just eat good food. You've got to talk about it too. And you've got to talk about it to somebody who understands that kind of food."
Kurt Vonnegut

Signature Tastes of VANCOUVER

"I should have no objection to go over the same life from its beginning to the end: requesting only the advantage authors have, of correcting in a second edition the faults of the first."
Benjamin Franklin

Steven W. Siler is a firefighter-cum-chef serving in Bellingham, Washington. Long marinated in the epicurean heritage of the Deep South, Steven has spent over 20 years (dear God has it been that long?!) in the much-vaulted restaurant industry from BOH to FOH to chef. In addition, he has served as an editor and contributing writer for several food publications. When not trying to shove food down his fellow firefighters' gullets, he enjoys sailing and sampling the finest of scotches and

wines, and has an irrational love affair with opera. He swears one day he will relive the above picture on the Gulf Coast with a good Will.

The Signature Tastes series of cookbooks is the one of the first of a series of culinary celebrations from Smoke Alarm Media, based in the Pacific Northwest. Smoke Alarm Media is named for another series of unfortunate culinary accidents at an unnamed fire department, also in the Pacific Northwest. One of the founders was an active firefighter. Having been trained as a chef, he found himself in the position of cooking frequently at the fire station. Alas, his culinary skills were somewhat lacking in using the broiler and smoke would soon fill the kitchen and station. The incidents became so frequent that the 911 dispatch would call the station and ask if "Chef Smoke Alarm" would kindly refrain from cooking on his shift. Thus Smoke Alarm Media was born.

SIGNATURE TASTES HIDDEN EATS TABLE FACTS BYGONE ERAS ART OF CULINARY DIPLOMACY VARSITY SUBLIME NECTAR

Signature Tastes of VANCOUVER

CPSIA information can be obtained at www.ICGtesting.com
Printed in the USA
LVOW05s0212171113

361593LV00012B/775/P